Ferns in Your Garden

Ferns in Your Garden

John Kelly

SOUVENIR PRESS

To Kenneth and Dolsheen Adlam
with thanks

First published 1991 by Souvenir Press Ltd,
43 Great Russell Street, London WC1B 3PA
and simultaneously in Canada

ISBN 0 285 630237

Printed and bound in Hong Kong by
Dah Hua Printing Co. Ltd.

Contents

List of Illustrations

COLOUR PHOTOGRAPHS

BLACK AND WHITE PHOTOGRAPHS

Preface

THIS IS not a learned treatise on ferns, neither does it come from the pen of a fern specialist or collector. I am just a gardener; one who is fortunate enough to be allowed to spend his life communicating about plants and gardens.

I have felt for a long time that ferns were too much the concern of their devotees and too little encouraged as arrows in the gardener's quiver. In this book I have tried to present the case for ferns as garden plants for everyone, in the hope that increased interest in them will lead not only to their proper appreciation, but also to the preservation of some of the most intriguingly beautiful but uncommon forms.

The nomenclature of ferns is infuriating. I cannot be alone, for example, in feeling total frustration at the constant indecision about the place of the hart's tongue in fern taxonomy. Either it is an asplenium or it is a phyllitis, so would the men and women in white coats please make up their minds. The question of cultivar naming is extremely vexed, and I must emphasise that my views are those of one who strives to understand, rather than to instruct.

I could not have written this book without being familiar with *Hardy Ferns*, Reginald Kaye's masterpiece. I have used it as a reference work and acknowledge its enormous value to me during the years since it was published in 1968, shortly after which Mr Kaye was kind enough to autograph my treasured copy.

I am also deeply indebted to Kenneth Adlam, who allowed me free rein in his superb Devon garden, in which the principles of growing ferns as garden plants are demonstrated to perfection. He and his wife, Dolsheen (Julia), showed me a warm and unaffected hospitality that I shall never forget.

My thanks also to Rosemary Norton of Ottery St Mary, Devon, England; Eleanor Phillips of Sherkin Island, Co. Cork, Ireland; Friedrich Vogel, father and son, of Kells Bay, Co. Kerry, Ireland; Tony Cohu; Eva Bean; Mr A. R.

Busby, Secretary of the British Pteridological Society; Gwladys Tonge; The Hon Charlotte Morrison of Abbotsbury, Dorset, England; The University Botanic Garden, Cambridge, England; The Irish National Parks Department and Finbarr O'Sullivan; The University Botanic Garden, Leiden, Holland; The Marie Selby Botanic Garden, Saratosa, Florida; and the Fairchild Tropical Garden, Coral Gables, Florida.

It goes without saying that my astonishing wife, Nicola, who built with her own hands the study in which I write and who goes so far as to read the product, is essential to the process.

John Kelly
The Borlin,
Co Cork, Ireland
and Pound Hill,
Sussex, England

1

Introduction to Ferns

YOU WILL find garden clubs or their equivalent in almost every country. What is fascinating about them is how diverse they are. There are rock garden clubs in Scotland and America, leek clubs in the north of England, and international societies and associations for almost everything from fuchsias to fenugreek.

In most cases the affections of members are directed towards plants that are colourful in flower, majestic in stature, or good to eat. Most people rightly expect beauty, style and brightness from a garden. In fact, there is perhaps a tendency for flower colour to be a little too much to the fore; it is arguable that we should pay more attention to the greenery and leafage which can so enhance the effects of flowers.

Few clubs or societies devote themselves to such matters, although flower-arrangers are notably conscious of foliage effects. However, lurking as it were among the lists of groups that specialise in flowering plants, there can be found those whose members are enthralled by ferns.

Some such people like to be pteridologists, but many refer to themselves in simple terms – as fern lovers or perhaps as fern specialists. Most, however, are just gardeners, and that is why they can make the most of ferns; their broad-mindedness allows them to treat ferns as plants among plants.

It is a pity that ferns have not been generally visualised as garden plants. Of course one is intellectually aware of their place in the scheme of things, but they have still tended to be seen as creations apart. The old description of something that did not fit neatly was 'neither fish, fowl, nor good red herring'. Ferns can be said to have been just such an anomaly in the plant world, fit neither for the boskage, the parterre, nor the good broad border.

Nevertheless, they were at one time the subjects of a craze and the objects of well-to-do collectors. Large, elaborate, wildly expensive, heated structures –

stove houses, conservatories, and above all 'ferneries' – were constructed during late Victorian and Edwardian days. In America, *Nephrolepis exaltata* was shipped north in large quantities from its home in the southern United States, there to forget its romps as ground cover and its cosy niches on the trunks of palms, to enter captivity and receive the slave name of 'Boston' fern.

Crazes are not only short-lived; their subjects are usually reduced finally to an obscurity that they otherwise might not have suffered. Attempts to bring back the feather boa, the hula hoop or flared trousers seem doomed to failure; there is an element of shame in the feelings of those who went overboard in the first place. Ferns, on the other hand, are in the position of the black bottom, dropped waistline, and the convertible. They were all so long ago, why not try them again?

That people should ask such a question is not very surprising. Who is there who has not appreciated the feathery coolness of ferns along a stream bank in summer, or stopped for a moment to admire their filigreed structure? They are restrained, modest plants for the most part, but is there not a role for such qualities in the garden?

There is, of course, but we have tended to lose sight of it as a result of the Victorians and their ferneries. The dank, dark, dripping dens, echoes only partly muffled by the lowering dicksonias and the ubiquitous moss, must have damped the ardour of many a couple who, slipping out from the dance for a moment, found clinging fronds less than encouraging.

Out of doors, their fern grottoes were exercises in grotesquerie, almost as if the nightmare quality of Snow White's forest were something to be admired. How sad it is that such a noble, gentle, and supremely lovely group of plants should have been reduced to melancholy, when their delicate charms are much more redolent of quiet joy.

The years of the First World War put paid to the fern craze. The *Grand Guignol* aspect disappeared as the expense of heated structures bit; families had less time for occupying their minds with relative trivia while each of them had someone to mourn – and anyway most of the gardeners were being lost for ever on the battlefields. Ferns do not take kindly to being overgrown, and soon weeds displaced them from the bizarre, fantastic rockeries upon which so many of them had been condemned to grow.

It was not until much later that it was realised that many ferns could thrive out of doors in the open garden. Some, like the common male fern, appeared fairly indestructible; others such as the soft shield fern seemed to renew their annual fronds without too much trouble. It took some working out to realise that ferns do not like becoming grimy and that many that had been deemed

Nephrolepis exaltata, the Boston fern, festooning the trunk of a palm tree. Marie Selby Botanic Garden, Sarasota, Florida. *John Kelly*

tender or difficult were, in fact, killed by pollution.

It is fashionable to imagine that our present environment is highly polluted. This is, of course, no bad thing if it concentrates our minds on the condition of our world. On the other hand, exaggeration leads to erroneous conclusions. The air in the industrialised western countries is far cleaner now than it was at any time during the first half of the twentieth century, and a wide variety of ferns can be grown in town gardens as well as in the country.

Clarity of thought about nature has played its part, too. Gardeners are now less likely than they used to be to take rules of thumb for granted. Neither will they accept gardening lore or horticultural dicta at face value. It is commonplace for people without formal scientific training to be found successfully applying scientific method to their gardening; they erect hypotheses or allow them to be erected, and then spend a lot of time enjoying themselves in trying to knock them down.

In this way many ferns have been found not to need the dark, wet places in which little else would grow. Refusal to believe it has led to experiment, and many of the trials have turned out successfully, proving the versatility of ferns, both as to surroundings and hardiness, to be impressive.

The Appeal of Ferns

Ferns are not flowering plants and, with very few exceptions, those that will grow in Cool Temperate gardens owe nothing of their charm to large stature or to any structures other then their fronds. If it is for their fronds alone that we grow them, what is it that makes them so attractive?

The quality of being ferny — of ferniness — is one that is praised in other plants. The finely pinnate foliage of the florist's mimosa, *Acacia dealbata*, that of the true *Mimosa pudica*, and the divided, canopy-forming leaves of *Aralia elata*, are all described approvingly as ferny. There is something in ferniness that is inherently alluring.

It is, perhaps, a combination of lightness and regularity. Fern fronds have a symmetry that is not often displayed in the foliage of higher plants. Palms have it, and so do cycads* — two other plant groupings that are in our gardens without qualifying on account of flowers.

This symmetry is evident even in species with simple fronds, such as *Asplenium scolopendrium*, the hart's tongue fern. The long, strap-shaped fronds are straight and uniform, and their heart-shaped bases, neatly distributed in a circle at the centre of the plant, create a symmetrical whole.

In ferns with compound fronds, the symmetry is more striking, since there

* An ancient family of somewhat palm-like plants, varying in size from about one to over twenty feet tall, members of which, along with ferns, horsetails and clubmosses, dominated the vegetation that went to make up our coal measures.

Athyrium filix-femina 'Fieldiae', delicate and graceful with its spare, arching fronds. University Botanic Garden, Cambridge. *John Kelly*

is, as it were, more of it. A simply pinnatifid frond (divided once into opposite segments, but not reaching the middle), such as that of *Polypodium vulgare*, is an immediately recognisable first step in ferniness, even though it is so elementary. A truly pinnate frond, with the pinnae (divisions) cut all the way to the midrib, is even more so.

When the pinnate stage is reached, the frond is recognisably ferny. However, further elaboration is possible, with symmetrical subdividing of the pinnae into smaller ones (bipinnate) and even a stage further (tripinnate).

All this subdivision makes for lighter and lighter structures, and it is these, contrasted with the shapes of other plants, particularly in heavy-looking plantings, that are an important part of the attractiveness of ferns. The contrast works the other way round, too, with the possibilities of using *Asplenium scolopendrium* a., a contrast with lighter ferns or with other plants altogether. It is, for instance, perfect as a bright, glossy green carpet beneath Japanese maples, where its colour and shapes make telling contrasts at all times of the year with the shapes and changing colours above.

It is hard to know how much of our love for certain things — scents, birdsong, the sun setting on sea — is founded on childhood experience. Certainly I remember walks in woods in North Wales, where ferns and primroses abounded, and trace my fondness for ferns to that, no less than my long-standing delight in primulas. It is not unlikely than an American from a northern State, conceiving a passion for ferns in later life, might, if he thought hard, discover that he had once walked among the two-foot fronds of *Dryopteris clintoniana* or met, as a child, the fascinating *Cystopteris bulbifera*.

With true fern fanciers the connection between the wild and the cultivated is strong. They will tramp the hills, penetrate the deepest hollows, and tolerate the most uncivilised weather in search of species or variants of species. It is to ferners of the past that we owe many of our garden forms, but we must thank them and move on along the road on which we have been set by our broader knowledge. The world is now our parish and we have beaten its boundaries: we have learned to study Nature where she lies and not to take bits of her home like prizes from school. Today's fern people look, marvel, photograph, and go home empty-handed but full of memories.

Besides, there is no more need to plunder the wild for ferns. We have the species, and there are so many varieties of them in cultivation that it takes many years of study before they are all grown and known by each gardener. Furthermore, the cultivated stock is constantly producing sporelings that are different from anything else. Sometimes one will be so good that it warrants a name and vegetative propagation, and a new garden form is born.

Collecting plants, except in the world's remote places, and then only by experienced plant hunters working with the approval of botanical institutes and governments, must be regarded as forbidden. Prohibited, that is, by the best form of legislation, the wishes of the great majority of the world's people. It is also, one is glad to say, increasingly subject to legal sanction.

Psychological and philosophical considerations aside, ferns provide the gardener with a 'leaf' structure that few other plants can offer. Those that come anywhere near ferns in prettiness of foliage, like some of the fennels, are invariably compared with and described in terms of ferns.

They are also so very green. There are many shades of green and ferns provide quite a few of them. They are so variously deep, tranquil, bright, lettucy, smudged with black, or just gorgeously fresh, that one has to say, simply, that they are beautiful.

The Names of Ferns

Everything about a fern that has been given to it by Nature is beautiful. Unfortunately, man's heavy hand has endowed ferns with names that are anything but lovely.

It is not possible to dwell on ferns without starting to use Latin nomenclature. Vernacular names are all very well, but 'hart's tongue' will mean little to a New Zealander, whose 'necklace fern' is unrecognisable to a Briton. Give the latter its Latin name, *Asplenium flabellifolium*, however, and everyone is talking the same language.

The romance of native names is undeniable. Who would not prefer 'silvery glade fern' to *Athyrium thelyopteroides*? Unfortunately, confusion soon sets in. The oak fern, for instance, is *Gymnocarpium dryopteris* and is not at all related to the American oak fern, *Onoclea sensibilis*, which is so called because of its resemblance to the foliage of an American oak. In a wider world of language, too, it becomes arrogant to insist on one's own vernacular.

The Latin names of ferns are worth mastering because of the wondrously ornamental nature of the plants themselves. The species are not so bad — each has its 'surname' first — but it is when the varieties are met with that a little patience is needed.

You might wish that you had not interested yourself in ferns at all when you come across names like *Polystichum setiferum* 'Pulcherrimum Bevis'. Persevere, though, as it is not as hard as it seems. In this example, *Polystichum* is the genus to which the shield ferns belong, while the specific epithet *setiferum* refers to the soft shield fern. So far you know that you are dealing with the shield fern with the soft, rather than leathery, fronds. The last words, printed in Roman type and bounded by single inverted commas, make up the cultivar name. A cultivar is a form arising in cultivation (i.e. not in the wild) which can be vegetatively propagated — by division in this case. Strictly speaking, cultivar names should be in the vernacular, but allowance is made for names which, like this one, are long-established.

The reason for the length and complexity of Latin parts of the names of some cultivated ferns is that there are many kinds that are just such variations from the simple species which, having been found in the wild in the first instance, come true from spores. You are not allowed to find one and call it 'Mrs Money-Baggs' in the hope of inheriting, neither should you call it after your spouse in a fit of misguided romanticism. It simply has to be given a supplementary name in Latin by someone recognised as a botanical authority on the species. Examples of these are *Blechnum penna-marina alpina* and *Botrychium australe millefolium*.

If your plant of a species or botanical variety produces a sporeling with notably different and horticulturally desirable characteristics, then you yourself are at liberty to call it 'Dora-Lee' or whatever you like within certain rules of propriety; you must propagate it and have it described in print first, though.

One good thing about fern names is that there are not all that many genera. With shrubs, for instance, there are thousands. Hardy fern genera that will concern the most ardent fans scarcely amount to fifty. Once you become

Above: *Polystichum setiferum* 'Pulcherrimum Bevis'. King's Gatchell, Ottery St Mary, Devon. *John Kelly*

Right: Today's gardeners can quite easily re-create something of the environment that existed before the coal measures were laid down. Fairchild Tropical Garden, Coral Gables, Miami, Florida. *Nicola Kelly*

involved with the delicate, fascinating complexity of the plants themselves, you are much less likely to find their names cumbersome, and you will become as willing to use them as you would those of dearly loved friends in, say, Poland or West Africa.

What Ferns Are

When dinosaurs dominated the world of animals, ferns were everywhere. Giant tree ferns, cycads and horsetails towered over the masses of smaller ferns. There were no flowers as we understand them, although the cycads were technically flowering plants. It is not surprising, then, that ferns occur all over the world's surface now, including some of the coldest regions, like Greenland and parts of the Antarctic.

Ferns have no pollen, no seeds, and a life-cycle that is unlike other plants (see Chapter 8). They have fine, fibrous roots, crowns from which the fronds arise, and organs on the fronds which are part of the reproductive process. They must have moisture in order for this process to work and they still retain a love of the humidity and shadiness that existed in the primeval forest.

That forest's floor was rich with decaying and decayed plant remains. The ferns from which today's plants have descended were among the smaller ones, even the tree ferns of New Zealand, Australia and the tropics. They would have enjoyed a humus-rich, vegetable soil with an open, fibrous structure, and would not have found their roots engulfed in sticky clays or the claggy messes that most of us allow to pass for garden soils.

They are not all shade lovers, however. The great diversity of habitat enjoyed by ferns is one of the things that makes them so valuable in gardens. Several species thrive in open, sunny places, but the soil is almost never dry. The balance between exposure and moisture is critical; plants provided with shade can survive drought, while those given ample moisture can often take a good deal of sun.

Perhaps the greatest adaptation to changing conditions is shown by the epiphytic resurrection fern of the southern United States, which dries up so thoroughly that it can hardly be seen. A good soaking soon revives it and it recovers in a seemingly miraculous manner, becoming fresh and green again quite soon.

The roof of the smithy in the English village in which I lived until recently was covered on its north slope with a colony of the rhizomatous common polypody, *Polypodium vulgare* (but see p. 158). This little fern had occupied the roof certainly since the nineteen-twenties, and probably for much longer. Every summer it would turn brown and shrivel. Sometimes, in years when no rain would fall for three months or more, one feared for its survival, but it always recovered. It lived on the decaying remains of its own fronds and upon whatever came by the bounty of birds or the wind. There were no plants on the southerly slope of the roof.

Ferns can grow on the trunks of trees – usually lodging in the forks – providing that the atmosphere is moist. Many tropical ferns, such as the spectacular stag's horns, are epiphytic, while some have even adapted to growing on cacti and are themselves succulent. In growing ferns you are not dealing with the wimps of the plant world; they are born survivors and will grow for you as long as you do not expect too much. A filmy fern, just a few cells thick, cannot be expected to live on the rock garden; neither would you plant the long-suffering polypody in a bog.

Although some species of ferns are widely distributed in the world – *Osmunda regalis*, for instance, occurs in England and the rest of Europe, from the eastern USA down to Uruguay, and in India and east Asia – the fern populations of different regions of the world show remarkably different characteristics. The tree ferns of Australasia, for example, have stout trunks, while those of the West Indies are so slender that they hardly look capable of supporting the noble heads of fronds. North American ferns are almost all deciduous, while Japanese hardy ferns are nearly all evergreen.

There is something strange about the British Isles, however, which so far goes unexplained. British ferns show a propensity for developing crested, tasselled, 'crisped', plumose and divisilobe forms that no others do. And that is not all. Foreign ferns, brought into cultivation in Britain, begin to develop 'fancy' shapes. You will not see the Boston fern exhibiting eccentricity in its native home. Some plants will be smaller than others, but that is about all the difference between one plant and another in places where it grows in colonies of many hundreds of plants. British-grown plants, however, are a different story, and forms have occurred which the Americans had not seen throughout history.

It is tempting to speculate on what it might be that has this effect. Could there be something about Britain that promotes eccentricity? Certainly it is an admired quality in British life. Perhaps the climate does it. A phenomenon that warrants a little more examination is the considerable radiation in the form of radon gas that emanates from the granite formations on which many British ferns grow, and seeps into houses in granite areas. Mutations, which is what many of these forms would appear to be, are not unknown where radiation is a factor.

Whatever the cause, the changes of form have given rise to some of the most remarkably beautiful plants of any kind in cultivation. It is among these that

Athyrium filix-femina 'Vernoniae'. University Botanic Garden, Cambridge. *John Kelly*

fern buffs find the deepest satisfaction and gardeners the most diverse shapes and effects with which to create exciting combinations of plants.

Ferns as Garden Plants

There is a tendency to see ferns purely as plants for the specialist, and to a certain extent this is reflected in their availability. Luckily it is becoming less marked and even some of the large garden centre chains can be found stocking a few ferns now and then. The horticultural trade, like any other, is likely to excuse lack of availability by citing lack of demand, and it must be said that it has a point. However, the more we press for a supply of ferns, the more they will become a commercial proposition.

Meanwhile, specialist nurseries, or those perhaps with an interested member of staff, continue to be the main source of commercial supply. Outside commerce, the garden clubs and societies, especially the fern societies, are the best sources of most cultivars and are likely to remain so.

What will increase the availability of the ferns not readily obtainable at the moment will be a realisation that they are true garden plants, capable of being grown by people who are not specialists. Such gardeners have simply taken the trouble to find out about their needs, and have found that they can take their places in the garden, often growing in the same conditions as other plants and complementing them in making a more complete garden picture.

Ferns need not be relegated to the dankest, rubbliest corners; neither need they be confined to the fernery, a concept that is a long time a-dying. The idea of putting ferns all together in a fernery, which for some reason was always to be constructed of rock, is only just passing from the literature. Even so, its legacy is that ferns are essentially for the rock garden, and this is equally nonsense.

One of the most sympathetic uses of ferns that I have seen was carried out in a small bed beyond the closed end of a domestic garage. It was but a stride across and perhaps two wide, and in it was a happy community of different kinds of small ferns, growing in the companionship of several species and varieties of erodiums and geraniums. The latter were, of course, members of the genus *Geranium*, and not the pelargoniums to which we lend the name.

The flowering plants of the two genera are notable for their finely-divided or lobed foliage in shades of green or grey. So are the ferns. The characteristics of the two plants complement one another, therefore, but there is also a strong element of contrast: one could not confuse a fern and an erodium. The flowers, arriving in a long succession from spring to autumn, provided all that could be desired as enhancements to the foliage picture, but it would have been complete without them for all that.

If you visit the garden of one of today's fern experts, you will find there will be special areas where ferns thrive mightily — stream banks, ditches, hedge bottoms, and so on — but every effort will have been made to integrate the plantings with those of other kinds of plants. Fern fanciers of the present-day kind are much too experienced in how Nature works not to want to echo her deployment of variety.

Similarly, every garden arrangement will be one in which opportunities are sought to use ferns. Droughty, sun-baked spots apart, the fern person will plant his favourites wherever a good home and the right company presents itself. You will find the garden of such a devotee to appear at first sight remarkably unspecialised, so well will he or she have understood that hardy ferns are garden plants and not mysterious entities that need cosseting by those gifted with certain magic powers.

The fern lover will be quite likely to be enjoying a challenge, however, and

Polystichum setiferum and *Dryopteris dilatata* in a naturally arranged planting with *Buphthalmum speciosum*. Clodagh, Sherkin Island, Co. Cork, Ireland. *John Kelly*

you will probably find a greenhouse and some frames in which other ferns, some of which may be cold hardy, live because they are unfitted for the open garden. Great expense is not necessary if you want to grow some filmy ferns or others that need constant, even moisture. Neither is it all that costly to enlarge your range by trying some that are perhaps at the margin of hardiness where you live. After you have built up a small stock of them, you will be bound to try one or two outside, and it is success with such experiments that enlarges our knowledge and appreciation of the possibilities of the garden uses of ferns.

The range of hardy ferns — which is to say those that can be grown in places where frosts are fairly frequent and moderately severe — is very wide indeed. It is worth remembering that snow is an insulator, and that ferns that find themselves living in a climate where the winter temperatures are very low may well be far more comfortable below a blanket of snow than we are above it. Aside from that, there are a great many ferns that are every bit as tough as any of the usual stalwarts of the Cool Temperate garden.

They are not difficult to grow, either, so long as their requirements for friable soils and not too dry a site are kept in mind. Once ferns are established they take little in the way of looking after. In a dry summer their root areas may need to be soaked with water from time to time and regular mulching with leaves is an excellent idea. Tidy gardeners may wish to remove the dead fronds from deciduous species and varieties.

There is really not much at all to prevent gardeners everywhere discovering just what it is they have been missing in not having ferns as part of their inventory of good garden plants. Once you have realised their potential and found how engrossing they are, as well as how delightful, you will never be without them again.

2

Ferns and Gardens

CURIOUSLY ENOUGH, it is the ability of ferns to enjoy conditions disliked by flowering plants, which leads them to play the role of improvers of the garden. One of the things that you will be persuaded of when first encountering ferns will be their usefulness in dark corners in the shade of trees or buildings, or where it is wet underfoot. Nothing is that simple, of course.

Soils and Situations for Ferns

Everything depends on the soil. The chances are that it will be far from ideal: it is only the minority of gardens that have lightish, friable, vegetable soils, and even in those the ferny places are usually sticky, compacted, and sour.

Ferns, like any other rooted plants, are unable to stand stagnancy. Water in plenty — even in excess — is one thing, but if it cannot drain away efficiently, it is quite another. Their fine roots cannot thrive in heavy stickiness either, so wherever you plant ferns you must make sure that the drainage is excellent.

It is wrong to suppose that good drainage and dryness are the same thing. A soil that is bone dry in summer can be the most muddy of quagmires in winter. The bank of a stream, where there is water constantly about the roots of the plants growing in it, will be better drained the steeper the bank and the faster the stream. It is not the water that is the problem in badly drained soils, it is the lack of oxygen and the build-up of poisonous substances.

Consequently, no matter how suitable a part of the garden may be in other respects, the first job is to make it well drained, and this means good old-fashioned digging and the incorporation of as much organic matter as you can possibly get hold of. A soil that has had dug into it leafmould, garden compost, spent mushroom compost (but be careful, as it contains chalk) or any other bulky, fibrous, semi-decayed material, will be given and will maintain an open, well-oxygenated structure, even when it is wet.

It is important, too, to avoid subsequent compaction. After you have planted up the soil, you will find that routine tasks encourage you to put your feet in the same places each time. The soil will become compacted, the growing roots will have nowhere congenial to go, and you will soon be back where you started. This is very much so in small gardens or in small areas of larger ones. The answer is to put in some stepping stones before you plant, and then use them to plant from. In that way your weight will be transmitted to the soil at many fewer pounds to the square inch, compaction will be negligible, the stones will retain water and coolness beneath them in a hot season, and you will know that you will always be able to reach the centre of each plant.

With the improvement in the soil that you have effected in order to accommodate your ferns, you will find that you have rendered it perfect for other plants. Primulas, both European and Asiatic, will be well suited, as will pulmonarias, whose entire, spotted or silvered leaves make a fine contrast to the fronds of smaller ferns. Dodecatheons will thrive where there is a little more light, and meconopsis will flaunt their hosts of broad, blue poppies before the deciduous ferns unfurl and take over.

You must know, however, how acid or alkaline your soil is. The hard fern, *Blechnum spicant*, loves moisture, and grows happily in wet ditches in the Lake District of England and in Ireland (where it is to be found associating happily with *Pinguicula grandiflora* at the edge of one of my fields). It hates lime with a passion and cannot tolerate basic, calcareous soils. On the other hand, it will take all the moisture you can give it, as long as the water is lime-free, and will stand up to dripping from overhead trees.

There are many other ferns that dislike lime, such as *Dryopteris dilatata* and *Osmunda cinnamomea*, but that is not a reason to think that your options will be all that limited if you have a calcareous soil. The list of ferns, starting with the many cultivars of *Asplenium scolopendrium*, which enjoy lime and limestone, is a very long one indeed.

The capacity of *Blechnum spicant* for tolerating drip from trees is shared by other forms. When you are making your garden-improving fern planting you can use it and others like *Phegopteris connectilis* (the beech fern) and *Dryopteris dilatata* to occupy spaces where primulas and such like would not survive. This means that you can maintain the natural appearance of a woodsy corner without having to prune overhanging branches.

Dryopteris dilatata is a British native, called the broad buckler fern. It is a good example of a fern that will tolerate conditions which would kill most

Top: A large clump of *Dryopteris affinis* with *Osmunda regalis* in the background. Bramble Cottage, Ottery St Mary, Devon. *John Kelly*

Bottom: *Blechnum spicant*, the hard fern, thrives in deep shade and wet soils and is impervious to drips from overhead trees. Bramble Cottage, Ottery St Mary, Devon. *John Kelly*

flowering plants and yet cannot stand bad drainage. I know a little colony of it right next to that most antisocial of plants, *Rhododendron ponticum.* It is constantly dripped on, almost totally shaded, and threatened with imminent starvation by the plundering rhododendron. Nevertheless it is perfectly happy. The reason for this is that the plants are growing on a rotten tree stump, no more than six inches above ground, but thus perfectly drained. The stump provides a larder, too.

One good thing the rhododendron is doing is to protect the ferns from wind. Ferns detest winds, which tear at their fronds and damage them, or irreparably bend the midribs down so that the fronds sprawl on the dirty ground. Wind is the enemy of the fern family as a whole, which cannot reproduce under its drying influence. It sucks the moisture from evergreen fronds in winter.

Aspect and Climate

If you go walking in hilly country, much of the landscape will be exposed. The sun beats down, the wind rips, and the rain lashes painfully. The plant life has to put up with all this as well. Some plants cope by growing as tight cushions or tussocks; some by having small, crowded leaves, and yet others by having thick skins, wax, or hairy coats on their leaves.

Ferns cannot take these precautions. By their very nature they are unable to be reduced to cushion form and their lack of woodiness leaves them with no defence against being thrashed about by wind and wounded by driving rain. And yet you will find plenty of ferns growing in the hills, and not merely on the shady slopes.

They will tend to be growing in hollows, crevices in rocks, and on the shady sides of rocks if those are also sheltered from wind. On slopes out of the prevailing wind you may well find them in more open positions where they receive more sun. The more you look at ferns in the wild, the more you come to understand the basic equation that governs their lives.

Existence for a fern is all to do with the balance of moisture and the absence of physical damage. A site that will support a fern must have more water the more sun it has; the more water there is, the faster the drainage must be. The more wind there is, the more water will be needed; conversely, drier places must be out of the wind. The more the wind prevails, the greater is the need for a withdrawn, sheltered position. A fern that is exposed to sun and wind will grow with a reduced frond area to compensate for moisture loss, but this reduction has limits below which the plant cannot exist. Species that are naturally small are best adapted to exposed positions.

A fern species colonises and spreads to become successful by means of its spores. Those that germinate in suitable places, where there is a working balance between sun, moisture and wind, and the soil is good enough, will grow and themselves spore. Those that do not, die. That is why ferns have such an enormous number of spores. The important thing is that there is not a prescribed, rigid formula; it is the balance that determines whether or not the plant will live.

Since there are ferns that are capable of colonising almost any kind of terrain, from a stone wall to a bog, it follows that it must be possible to grow them in a very wide range of garden habitats. This is so, and exploiting the fact is a matter of applying your knowledge of the factors involved and seeing that you plant your ferns where they will most nearly find themselves in familiar conditions, as close to nature as you can possibly manage. You don't slavishly copy nature — you work out how she operates and apply the principles. It was failure to appreciate this that gave rise to the segregated ferneries of the past and stopped ferns from becoming the true garden plants that they are today.

Ferns are among the plants that are most sensitive to microclimates. These are highly local variations on the climate that prevails over a particular area. The word is often misused to denote a climatic variation involving a whole neighbourhood, or district. Its meaning is much more precise than that and has to do with the conditions in a very small area, like a particular garden or even a small corner of it; microclimates are often a function of height above sea level or height above the ground. They can be created by small but constant volumes of water, such as a mere bowl that is kept full.

The general climate of your area will largely determine what plants you can grow. This will be modified by the amounts of sun and wind that your garden receives or that it keeps out. At an even more local level, your garden may have features that render it more or less friendly to plants than others nearby.

A cold, sticky soil, for instance, reduces the length of the growing season. If your garden is in a hollow it may hold cold air and be a frost pocket. If it is open to winds from cold quarters (the east in the British Isles, the west in the eastern United States) it will support only the hardiest plants. If it generally faces south it will be warmer than one facing north.

Within that general garden climate microclimates are created by garden engineering and by plants. Thorough cultivation of the soil and the addition of large amounts of organic matter will warm it up. If it is sticky, it is warmed by making it less so; if it is sandy, the organic matter will make it retain more heat. Windbreak planting will make all the difference in the world to a garden plagued by wind. And if your aspect is a cold one — if you face north or east — make

A moist ferny border. University Botanic Garden, Cambridge. *John Kelly*

your beds wedge-shaped so that the northern or eastern sides are raised. This means that the beds will face in the direction opposite to the general one, and they will be much warmer.

Planting and Nutrition

When it comes to the question of feeding ferns, it pays once again to take a look at what happens in nature. In the wild, as often as not, their roots feed on the decaying remains of fallen leaves. As we have seen, they tend to huddle in wind-sheltered places which are just the sort of niches where blown leaves collect and form into a mulch.

Of course, we witness nature at a discrete and irrelevant moment in time; what we see is but a twinkling instant in the history of the bit of soil that is supporting the plants. The reality of the garden is quite different; we have no choice but to have a starting point. The trick is to make it relevant to the ferns' desired environment. In other words, we need to realise that a fern must feel as though its soil has always been suitable and has not just recently been made so. That is why, whether the soil of the garden needs improving physically or not, we should incorporate as much *well-rotted* organic matter as possible. From then on it is perfectly reasonable for mulches of much more intact material, such as partly broken down and even entire leaves to be used, because we have given the soil a past as well as a present.

This all applies to most plants and is good garden practice — sadly, not all that often applied — but with ferns mulching has extra benefits. It helps a great deal in preventing moisture loss from the soil and in preventing the soil's becoming frozen. This last is the worst enemy of the evergreen fern. Fronds that are open to the air and losing water, while unable to be supplied by the roots, are sentenced to death.

Mulching also prevents the plants from being splashed by soil when it rains. This is not just disfiguring; it will eventually kill a fern if it is repeated too often. Many ferns have roots that grow near the soil surface, and they will not only be fed but protected by a couple of inches of cool, moist organic material.

Planting is best carried out in spring or early autumn. These are the times when the soil is either warming up or still has some weeks of warmth left in it. In both cases root growth will continue after planting and the ferns can establish themselves before winter cold or summer heat and dryness induce stresses that would be too much for newly planted stock.

When planting, it is a good measure to fork in a fairly informal handful of bonemeal where the plants are to go. Four ounces to the square yard seems to be the consensus of opinion as to dose, and I would not argue with that except to confess that, apart from when fertilising lawns, I have never weighed out any material in my life. Perhaps I should start — who knows?

The application of bonemeal, which is a first-class, slow-release fertiliser, becomes even less scientific when, as it should be, it is added to your annual spring mulch. You won't need much — a double handful to a large barrow-load if you are a man, two for a woman, is plenty — but that is about as precise as you can be.

Ferns will never develop properly if they are crowded. Not only will the competition for food be too great; they will not display themselves well. Obviously you need to give larger ferns more room than smaller ones, but nobody can draw up a table of planting distances. Besides, it will depend on so many other factors, like sun, wind, temperature and rainfall, that it would be invidious to do so. However, if you give everything except the smallest a full square yard and two for the biggest (the tree ferns, of course, require a lot of room), you will not go far wrong.

It is not a good idea to use chemical fertilisers with ferns. They don't happen in nature. Ferns are perhaps the most nature-loving of all plants apart from

Polystichum setiferum 'Pulcherrimum Druery'. In the left foreground is *Blechnum penna-marina*; to the right is *Polystichum munitum*. King's Gatchell, Ottery St Mary, Devon. *John Kelly*

some high alpines, and they hate to feel that they have found themselves in a garden equivalent of a hamburger joint. Animal manure is quite all right, so long as it is really well rotted. Manure younger than two years is likely to cause root burning, and even three-year-old manure should be used sparingly in mulches. Its best use in quantity is in the initial ground preparation; after that, the aim is to produce a sturdy plant, well nourished of course, but not so overfed that it becomes soft and over-indulged, to fall prey to any passing frost or capricious wind.

I am not convinced of the benefits of peat. Undoubtedly it is a superb soil-conditioner, especially when thoroughly mixed dry with the soil and then soaked. The trouble is that I feel more and more that it is a non-renewable resource which we should treat with respect. This is more than the anxiety of a citizen of a country for which peat has always been a support of life — I have used far too much of it myself. It is a belief that the huge demand for it will shortly end the supply and we should, while regarding it as a legitimate aid to gardening, be a little less cavalier about it.

More to the immediate point, peat is very acid and there are genera of ferns that do not like acid conditions. Leaf mould does not worry such ferns, especially beech mould, which concentrates alkaline salts in its tissues.

It is not often appreciated that peat has no food value until it starts to break down. It is short on all soil minerals and is not, as many people suppose, composed of humus. Humus is a black, colloidal gel and is not fibrous at all. Peat is a humus precursor. Leaf moulds contain minerals, and if the one you use has a little less than it should of one or another of them it will not be enough to worry a fern. If there is one thing a fern expects from its soil (complete with its past, to which peat cannot contribute), it is humus.

Watering

Plants with such an affinity for moisture would seem to present special problems with watering, but this is not really so. Well-sited ferns in suitably improved soils will not suffer from drought as quickly as, say, a clump of delphiniums in the usual standard of border soil that one sees generally. Naturally, it is sensible to keep a sharp eye open, but the plants to take special care of are those that are newly planted.

When you plant a fern it is a good idea to soak the planting hole first. In fact, it is quite a good idea to do it with water that is fairly hot. If you wait a few seconds before planting you will do no harm, but the bottom heat that you trap may well help to get new roots moving. This is, I believe, a trick beloved of old-time Scots head gardeners; besides, it is a wonderful excuse for making a cup of tea.

Once you start growing ferns in pots — and you will if you do any propagating — watering becomes a little more tricky. Every authority I have ever read has counselled against the watering of lime-hating (calcifuge) plants with water containing lime. It would appear to be wise advice, founded on sheer common sense, and reinforced by the belief that the calcium salts are concentrated in the compost. I have to add that many of these authorities have been known to me personally and I have the greatest respect for them.

However, this is a book about personal experience and I have to say that I spent a dozen years running a large garden in which many thousands of lime-hating plants — autumn gentians, camellias, rhododendrons, azaleas, and many more — were all watered when in pots with the local water. It was so limy that the life of a kettle was little more than three years and water, left to stand for twenty-four hours, rendered the glass opaque. Not one plant suffered the slightest adverse symptom in all that time. The mist propagator used the same water,

and camellia and azalea cuttings were taken in July and kept in their trays until the following March.

I am, therefore, unable to concur with the advice of my peers and betters that ferns in pots should always be watered with rainwater in districts where the water supply contains calcium salts. The reasons why I make such a point about it are that it is expensive and inconvenient to set up a system of rainwater catchment, it is seldom that you have enough in a dry summer, and if you have never smelt the vile stink of a water butt that has not been completely proofed against the ingress of leaves and other matter that might decay as the level drops, the heat increases, and fermentation takes place, you cannot imagine how dreadful it is.

Given all that, it must surely be a relief to be told that it is unnecessary in the first place.

The lady fern, *Athyrium filix-femina*, happily sharing the habitat of rhododendrons and large deciduous trees. University of Leiden Botanic Garden, Holland. *John Kelly*

3

Ferns in Pots, Containers, and Conservatories

FERNS ARE ideal for growing in containers in small courtyard gardens that are shaded and where many other plants will not be happy. There are gardens like this in the centres of large cities that are sheer works of art, conjuring up in the most unpromising places atmospheres redolent of the jungle or rain forest.

To overdo the fern element in such a situation is as bad as to have too much of anything in a small space. What should be aimed for is a series of contrasts and comparisons, punctuated with splashes of colour in due season, but altogether harmonious.

City Gardens

It is not always realised that the winter temperature in a metropolitan city may very well be as much as ten degrees Fahrenheit warmer than in the surrounding countryside. This is even more pronounced than it used to be, as heat is trapped by the pall of exhaust emissions, escapes from heating systems, and is simply radiated and convected away from the massive array of homes and offices, many of which are recognised, if only by country people, as being markedly overheated.

City gardens are sheltered, too. You may not think so as you struggle to preserve your sight from flying objects as a gale howls down Regent Street or makes the World Trade Center swing like twin pendulums, but compared to a full-blooded blast out of the cold heart of a continent, untamed by the drag and filter of buildings, it is no contest.

This city climate — for it is a distinct one — will allow ranges of plants to be grown that are only possible in the mildest of country gardens. What is more, because your garden may be small and paved, its soil irredeemably soured, or perhaps because you have realised the potential of growing plants in pots, your garden may very well be containerised, thus allowing you to move some of the inhabitants indoors during cold periods. If it is impossible to do this, you can protect the more tender plants with sacking or the finest grade of plastic netting, such as is used for shading greenhouses.

It is for reasons such as these that one of the most effective of London's garden designers uses tree ferns without hesitation. Whereas country-grown *Dicksonia antarctica* can only be found far to the west, in Cornwall, the coast of Scotland, and Ireland, it is by no means uncommon in Chelsea or Westminster. Miraculously, *Cyathea* species, impossible except in the far south of Ireland, thrive there too.

American cities are so diverse in their climates that it is impossible to generalise except to say that tree ferns are unlikely to accept either burning heat or freezing. In Zones 9 and 10 they can, of course, be grown in the open garden in some shade. However, the soft shield fern, *Polystichum setiferum*, a plant for Zone 8, can be upgraded, if that is the term, in much the same way as tree ferns in London, England. It and the Japanese holly fern, *Cyrtomium falcatum*, another that is hardy in Zone 8, may not be as spectacular as dicksonias and cyatheas, but their evergreen fronds, well managed, can decorate the patios of north-eastern cities.

Dicksonias grow large in time in gardens. To see a stand of hundred-year-old specimens, their fronds spanning twelve feet and their trunks anything up to twenty feet high, is one of the pinnacles of one's gardening life. The radiating fronds, bipinnate, break up the incident sunlight so that anyone standing beneath them is subject to nature's out-crafting the art of the jeweller or the cunning of the filigree-worker. Such large specimens are not possible in cities, but they are, even when much smaller, among the masterpieces of the plant world.

The trunks are fibrous and have roots growing downwards among the old frond bases. For this reason they must be kept moist, and a daily spraying is called for in pot-grown specimens. Unfortunately, you will not be likely to experience the full joys of their adulthood, but it is by no means uncommon for tree ferns of four feet or so in height to grow successfully in containers that remain movable.

If you are fortunate enough to persuade one to grow larger than this, you do not have to face finding a good home for it somewhere else. You will need first to summon up whatever reserves of courage you have, after which you can cut off the fern's top to whatever length of trunk you want and plant the whole thing in a new pot as a cutting. If its fronds and stem are kept sprayed it will,

The tender tree fern, *Cyathea novae-caledoniae*, is a plant for the specialist in tropical ferns, or the skilful city gardener. Other species are hardy in very mild, moist areas. Fairchild Tropical Garden, Coral Gables, Miami, Florida. *Nicola Kelly*

astonishing as it may seem, root quite easily in a shady place in summer.

Dicksonia fibrosa is a slighter plant and less often seen, but it is similar in many respects. When it is decapitated the old trunk may be retained, as young shoots may appear round it and make a mini-forest of young tree fern fronds.

It is not only in large cities that tiny, enclosed gardens are to be found, and while they may not be as warm as their town counterparts, provincial sites are not all that different when it comes to plant associations. Just a few ferns, but of the types that are immediately recognisable as typically ferny, are much better than too many of the crested or tasselled kinds, although one fern that I would never exclude is *Dryopteris affinis* (syn. *borreri*) 'Cristata The King'. This is a superb fern with militarily regular fronds that are pinnate. Each one is two or three feet long and ends in a neat crest, so that the plant combines a naturally ferny look, which is the note you want to strike, with just that amount of restrained artificiality of form that is appropriate in the formality imposed by walls or fences. It lends itself to container culture, since it is never so effective

Angiopteris evecta, a tender tropical fern from Malaysia, has the largest frond seen in the world. Fairchild Tropical Garden, Coral Gables, Miami, Florida. *Nicola Kelly*

as when reduced to just one crown, and therefore does not have to be big to excel.

Indeed, the smaller ferns are highly desirable in pots and containers, not only on their own account, but also as accompaniments to the larger ones. A large number of ferns are natural epiphytes – which is to say that they grow on the trunks or branches of trees – so it is by no means inappropriate to encourage this. Unfortunately, the species of *Pyrrhosia*, a genus of delightful New Zealand epiphytes that are hardy in cities and sheltered places, are rarely obtainable unless within a fern society, but the common polypody, *Polypodium vulgare*, or its near relative, *P. australe*, will grow equally happily on the trunk of a tree fern or at the feet of any other large cousin.

Tender Ferns

Although this is a book about ferns as garden plants, and therefore primarily to do with the ones that can be grown in the open garden or courtyard in Cool Temperate gardens, it is hard to draw lines across fern culture and exclude certain aspects of it.

Once you develop an interest in and fascination for ferns, you are unlikely to prohibit yourself from growing them in the house, and you are highly likely to advance into the realms of growing tender, or marginally tender, ferns under glass. Eventually you may find yourself deeply involved with rarities and difficult ferns, and it is a good idea to have some notion of how far such things can go.

Growing the sorts of ferns that need greenhouse treatment can be very expensive, often heartbreaking, and is an activity that really only comes with expertise in ferns generally. Those who find themselves challenged by the chanciness of growing filmy ferns will be entering an esoteric world, but one that can be enjoyed in the smallest space when you know how, while others, intrigued, perhaps by the prospect of growing *Angiopteris evecta* — the largest non-tree fern in the world — might consider taking out a further mortgage.

However, as house plants, ferns offer many possibilities and are not difficult, so long as the principles of good drainage and exclusion of draughts are constantly remembered. The Boston fern, remarkably tough for a native of Florida, is an all-time favourite and will remain so as long as its price does not become too high. That it has stood the upheaval of a climatic change says a lot for it, and it is by no means a difficult plant. Some of the less hardy Maidenhair ferns — *Adiantum* species — are quite easy too. These need constant moisture but no hint of waterlogging, and the only other attention they require is that their old fronds should be cut away as they become dry and discoloured.

Draughts and dry air are the main enemies of house plant ferns. This applies to all of them and they show their resentment by turning yellow and dying back. It is quite remarkable how difficult many people find indoor ferns; the average lifespan of most of the plants that are produced by the large wholesale firms can be measured in days, rather than weeks.

Apart from the Boston fern (*Nephrolepis exaltata*) and its several crisped (ruffled) and plumose (cut into fine filaments) varieties, it is the forms of *Adiantum raddianum*, a maidenhair fern from Brazil, that are the most widely grown. They can be found in any florist's shop or garden centre, and are good value for money. All they ask is that they should not receive direct sun, but adequate light, and a place that is cool, but not cold, and totally free of draughts. Central heating that is persistently turned up too high is death to them.

It is often maintained that house plant ferns should be frequently sprayed with tepid water in order to maintain high humidity. This is just not true. A moment's thought, anyway, will be enough to establish that you would have to

A stag's horn fern (*Platycerium bifurcatum*) hanging in a small, frost-free greenhouse. King's Gatchell, Ottery St Mary, Devon. *John Kelly*

be forever spraying, as it does not take long for the moisture on and around the fronds to evaporate and swiftly be dispelled into the general atmosphere in the room. The fact is that living rooms in most modern houses tend to be far too humid anyway, in spite of a widespread belief to the contrary, mainly due to room temperatures that are far too high and cause distortion of 'green' wood. When consideration is given to the amount of water vapour given off by a warm human being and this is set alongside the lack of ventilation that is almost universal, it is not surprising that the fern that arrives as a house present soon turns its toes up.

The same considerations apply to the 'table' ferns — mostly forms of *Pteris cretica* — that are popularly grown in houses. They are attractive plants of simple frond construction, sometimes crested, but they are apt to become boring after a while.

The gardener who is really interested in ferns is, perhaps, unlikely to grow popular house plant ferns for very long, as his sense of adventure will soon get the better of him. He is likely to want to use the house as an adjunct to the garden — even as an annexe to the conservatory — and to grow in it the plants that fascinate him but which he cannot accommodate elsewhere.

For example, my wife has become greatly fascinated by stag's horn ferns. I do not know what it is about them, but whenever she sees one she is stopped in her tracks, her attention riveted to their strange, primeval fronds that are like nothing else. There are two species that are reasonably easily obtained, *Platycerium superbum* and *P. bifurcatum*. They are pure epiphytes, and the better of the two for the house is *P. bifurcatum*, as it prefers a cool, 'normal' atmosphere, whereas *P. superbum* enjoys tropical temperatures and very high humidity (but not the rough and tumble of the living room, its humid atmosphere notwithstanding).

A log, about nine inches in circumference and a foot long, still with its bark attached, is cut vertically in half — that is, the cut goes on the diameter. The fern will probably have arrived in a pot, from which it is removed. The round ball of fibrous roots is then wrapped in moist sphagnum moss and attached to the bark with lightweight horticultural wire, preferably of the kind that is encased in plastic. The log is hung with its flat (cut) surface against a wall, and the plant then takes what nutrients it needs from the air, the light, and the water it is given at intervals by being dunked, log and all, in tepid water.

I fear it will not be long before my wife decides to try her hand at filmy ferns. They are in general plants of the Tropics, but one or two are native to colder countries, including the British Isles. Even so, they are tender in the sense that, while capable of tolerating low temperatures, they are extremely vulnerable to the slightest degree of dryness. Frost kills them. Their fronds are only one cell thick, so they must have one hundred per cent humidity, or as near to it as can be managed. Growing them is one of the more *recherché* branches of gardening, but if you try a version of the wardian case, you can have a lot of fun with them in the house.

A wardian case is only an enclosed glass tank. It was devised by Nathaniel Ward during the nineteenth century and transformed plant collecting, in that plants that would otherwise have died from desiccation could be transported over long distances in a humid environment.

Filmy ferns are not the sort of thing that you can pick up on a Sunday afternoon trip to the garden centre, but your ferny friends will put one or two your way when you have your feet under their table, so it is as well to know in advance how to deal with them.

The common tropical fish tank that you buy from the local pet store is as good as anything. Some authorities recommend making draining holes in the bottom and allowing the tank to stand in a tray to catch the excess water. I have found this to be unnecessary — well, what I really mean is that I have had success without doing it — and have made them up using about two inches of washed gravel at the bottom. On top of that, an inch of granulated charcoal keeps everything sweet and promotes an aerobic soil environment, and then a layer of sphagnum moss acts as a moisture reservoir and prevents the compost from fouling the lower layers. Finally, a good two inches of fibrous fern compost, worked among a few rocks to make it interesting, completes the set-up. The usual metal hood can be dispensed with in favour of a sheet of glass.

The general idea is that it is a self-perpetuating system, in which evaporation condenses and returns to the soil. A good watering should last for weeks. Of course, it is vital that the case be kept out of the sun, but good light is essential.

Water, in the shape of a tiny pool or miniature waterfall, provides added interest. In one of the pavilions in the Keukenhof, at Lisse, in Holland, this is done in a fascinating way that could perfectly well be emulated at home. The tanks there are planted vertically, so that you look at a garden that appears to be on the wall. A gentle fall of water runs down some smooth rocks, and the ferns are planted on ledges among them. The water ends up in a pool, from which a miniature electric pump returns it to the top. The little gardens are artificially lit. Several species of small, moisture-loving ferns are grown in them and they thrive beautifully.

Such an arrangement would be a delightful decoration for a room, as well as a perfect environment for the plants, especially when the lighting allows them to be placed in a darker part of a room.

The filmy ferns are mostly found in New Zealand, and you may well come across some of the species. Among British ferns, two filmy species exist, while there is one in the Republic of Ireland with outliers in Wales and Scotland. To grow these is to strike a blow for conservation, so long as you obtain them in cultivation and *not* in the wild. The Killarney station for *Trichomanes speciosum* is now secret because of past depredations by unscrupulous collectors, but those who can keep it going in cultivation, along with *Hymenophyllum wilsonii*, from the western districts of Britain, are doing Nature a service.

All the species of *Asplenium*, including *A. scolopendrium*, the hart's tongue fern, are suitable for the wardian case treatment. With the latter you would be advised to restrict its use to larger tanks, as it can grow to be quite large. It is, of course, totally hardy, but its appearance sits well with the more exotic inhabitants. The same goes for *Asplenium trichomanes*, the maidenhair spleenwort, which I have grown in England in the humidity of a tropical fish tank; a far cry from the south-facing wall of my stables in Ireland.

Potting Composts

Whether your ferns are thoroughly hardy ones that you want to grow in containers for convenience, or rather exotic ones that you feel you need to have under your complete control, the composts in almost all cases will be the same. This is simply because the needs of ferns are similar all over the world; at the risk of becoming repetitious, these are perfect drainage, leafiness, and a good

proportion of well-rotted vegetable matter.

Ideally, well decomposed leaf litter (leaf mould) should be used, in combination with loam and sand. Quite honestly, this is a counsel of perfection for most of us, especially those in cities, for whom potting is probably more important than for anyone else. What is more, leaf mould is not exactly plentiful in Islington, London, or Queens, New York. We will probably have to use peat, in which case a coarse, fibrous sphagnum peat should be used, or composted tree bark.

I confess to not having tried bark in fern composts, but believe that we may have to if our collective environmental conscience puts enough pressure on us. Other alternatives to peat, like coconut fibre, sound interesting, but time will tell. Meanwhile, I shall continue to advocate peat until the substitutes have been thoroughly tested.

The loam fraction, too, is not so easy. Where do you get it from if you have a small city yard? And do you really want to clutter the place up with coarse sand? The answer is to buy a John Innes type loam-based compost and add it to twice its bulk of fibrous peat. On no account use sedge peat (which is greasy) or poor, powdery grades of sphagnum peat. Lime-hating ferns will not be troubled by the lime fraction in J.I. composts; the acidity of the peat will take care of that.

It is a great mistake to use too large a pot. Soil without roots in it to take up the moisture soon becomes sour. For this reason it is probably better to start off with as large a plant as you can afford or with three or so, which you can put into the same pot. Small pots dry out quickly, so if you are out at work all day you may find them a worry; finding a justifiable way of using larger ones is a considerable help.

Potting-on is easy provided the plants have not been allowed to become pot-bound. A fern that has over-filled its pot with roots will not pot on well, as the roots will be unlikely to advance into the new compost. The best thing is not to let it happen; the second best is to remove the plant from its pot and gently roll the rootball on the surface of the potting bench. Gradually it will begin to break down and release what soil there is among the roots. You can then gently tease the roots out and repot, working new compost among the roots as you go. Once again, do not be tempted to pot on into too large a container. You can't accelerate nature and your patience will be rewarded by grateful plants.

Fern fanciers used to swear by clay (terra cotta) pots. I am sure they were right and have always preferred them myself. For decorative effect they have no peers, and there are now some very beautiful ones on the market, albeit fairly (and, I am certain, justifiably) costly. However, there is no need to worry

The 'wardian case' effect. The sea spleenwort (*Asplenium marinum*) growing under a bell-jar in a frost-free greenhouse. If the jar is removed for more than a minute or two it could be fatal to the fern, but in this case both the fern and its owner recovered. King's Gatchell, Ottery St Mary, Devon. *John Kelly*

about plastic pots. They are perfectly adequate and nowadays are well designed. You should not concern yourself with crocking pots, either. Clays benefit from an inverted piece of broken pot over the drainage hole, but who wants to break a pot to provide crocks these days? A disc of perforated zinc will do the job that is wanted, which is to prevent the egress of compost through the drainage hole. This does not happen with the much smaller, more numerous holes in plastic pots.

The whole idea of crocking was erroneous, anyway. The crocks took up valuable space which could have been occupied by nutritious compost, and besides, it flew in the face of the facts of gravity. If the drainage is unimpeded — if the compost's structure is such that it is *ipso facto* well drained — what goes up must come down.

Companion Plants for Ferns in Pots

If you are a city gardener and find yourself with a small, shady, sheltered garden or yard, in which you decide to grow containerised ferns, you will feel the need to exercise your colour sense as well as your feel for form, shape, and greenness.

Assuming that you go for a fairly jungly effect — which is irresistible in such circumstances, as it tends to blot out the surroundings and create an inner world of peace so much at variance with the near-insanity outside — you should let other plants join in and even enhance the atmosphere you are endeavouring to create.

Among leafy plants, *Fatsia japonica*, totally different in form from any fern with its large, hand-like, upturned leaves, is just right. It suits the ambience but creates contrast, and it provides a tropical note while at the same time being a hardy plant. There is a variegated form with white edges to the leaves that is most attractive and accentuates the contrast. Clusters of white flowers like shirt studs (are there still such things?) a rive in autumn, just when they are wanted.

If your ferny place is mild enougl or if you have room to bring plants in for winter, you can grow the New Zeala d cordylines to great effect. Their bunches of long, stiff, sword-like leaves on hort trunks make a great contrast to the filigree of the ferns and to the broad leaves of a fatsia. They are called cabbage palms, although they are not palms at all, but relatives, strangely enough, of the lilies. The true cabbage palm, if such a thing exists, is the state tree of Florida, but it is too tender outside a glasshouse away from the Sub-Tropics. Instead, the Chinese Chusan palm, another fan palm and of better shape, can remain outside in all but the coldest climates. Its main enemy is wind, not cold,

Woodwardia radicans planted at the foot of a shady wall in a very mild garden. Ilnacullin, Garinish Island, Co. Cork, Ireland. *John Kelly*

and the sheltered natures of the enclosed yards we are talking about are perfect for it.

The Chusan palm is *Trachycarpus fortunei*. It takes many years for it to exceed six feet in total, leafy height, but it gives good value early on, as true palms make their circumferences before they grow significantly upwards. Its trunk is covered in a fibre which is, unbelievably, actually woven by Nature, so much so that it is used for rough clothing in parts of China.

Cordylines flower in summer, with great plumes of tiny white stars. It has generally been maintained that *Cordyline australis* is the hardiest, but in fact the much more exotic-looking *C. indivisa*, whose leaves are three times as wide and almost twice as long, is turning out to be hardier, as plants from seed gathered from colder provenances prove their worth.

Given a good framework of strong foliage, branches and trunks, all conspiring to create your mini-jungle and further sheltering your ferns as they provide a symphony of textures in green below and among them, you can introduce colour. The exotic can be welcomed with open arms, but harmony will not be achieved if sun lovers from dry places, like zonal pelargoniums, are introduced.

The sorts of flowers that go with a close, intimate, private fern fantasy are ones that have a tropical, steamy feel about them. Fuchsias, for example, hanging like so many frilly lanterns, are ideal. They enjoy dampness (but not sogginess) and prefer the coolness of a ferny atmosphere to the heat of the sun. A shrub that has something of the same effect is the Chilean *Crinodendron hookeranum*, whose linear, dark green foliage is totally unlike that of fuchsias, but whose flowers are quite fuchsia-like in their lantern-like shape, dangling habit, and red colour.

Strelitzias, the bird-of-paradise flowers, grown in shelter in winter and put out among the ferns and their allies after the frosts, are tropical enough, but the greatest triumph I have seen was a planting of pleiones on the mossy slopes of the edge of a pool. These are terrestrial orchids, only a couple of inches tall, but with flowers as large and brightly coloured as cymbidiums. They are hardy, too, but people usually grow them in pots and lift them for dry storage during winter. They grow from pseudobulbs, flask-shaped organs that love to sit with their round bottoms in damp moss and their tapered bodies above it.

In a tiny garden in Boulogne-Billancourt, a suburb of Paris, I saw them flowering like pink and purple butterflies at the edge of a fern-girt pool. Maidenhair ferns attended them and were in turn leaned over by others, their pots cunningly hidden or blended in among the general greenery. There was no one to ask about them; their owner must have been out at work and I was myself trying to obtain directions to a fairly urgent appointment. I drank in the sight and moved on, the advancing tread of a policeman towards my illegally parked car ensuring that my camera did not see the light of day. I live in the deep, wild countryside and would not attempt such a joyful gardening cameo, but perhaps you could.

In the truly open garden the possibilities for combining ferns with flowering plants are almost endless. In your small, urban, even metropolitan enclave you must make your picture with a few economical, perfectly chosen strokes. To have the large white trumpets and dizzy scent of *Mandevilla suaveolens*, the Chilean jasmine, threaded about and over your ferns and their friends is to create the unforgettable. To introduce nasturtiums is to perpetrate the unforgivable.

Conservatories

A wardian case or converted fish tank is a way of enjoying ferns if you have no garden at all, or it is a means whereby you can grow the most testing of them that would not stand up to any other kind of treatment. However, tenderness in ferns does not mean that they all have to be sequestered in the horticultural equivalent of an intensive care unit. If you have a conservatory, you can widen considerably the range of ferns that you can grow, and you can use them in what amounts to a garden context.

A conservatory used to be a rather pompous addition to a house. It had small, overlapping panes of glass, thick wooden frames, finials and wavy bits all over the place, and was heated by a coal-burning boiler and big iron pipes. Large conservatories often became ferneries, as we know, but the modern conservatory, lightly built and full of light, is a different sort of place altogether. The panes of glass are large, the frames slender, and the light transmission superb. It is not necessary to provide much heat; in fact a minimum temperature of 45 degrees F is as much as is needed to allow a very wide range of plants to grow and a considerable fraction of the heat that is necessary to attain that level is provided by the wall of the house.

An illustration of this conducting effect is provided by a 'Paul Crampel' pelargonium that grew in my conservatory in the English Midlands for many years. It was right up against the house wall, where it provided annually a home for a family of thrushes and had to be pruned with a billhook. The outside temperatures not infrequently fell to 10 F, and there was no heating in the conservatory.

In fact, an unheated conservatory will support quite a wide range of tender ferns and other plants, but it is much safer to have heat on tap in case of unusual or prolonged cold.

There are two ways of using plants in a conservatory. You can either plant them directly into beds or grow them in pots. It is probably the best idea to grow in pots just those plants that you will want to move outside during the warmer weather — dicksonias and so on — and plant the permanent residents in beds. When you have your summer furniture deployed you will need the space to be uncluttered; in winter the conservatory can take on more of a storage role.

In the conservatory beds, ferns must be planted with other kinds of plants, otherwise the worst elements of the fernery will take over and dankness, dampness, and a boring sameness will soon make you wish you had not bothered. What needs to be remembered is that a conservatory has sharp gradients of internal climate; at ground level it may be cool and moist, while just under the glass may be hot and much drier. This does not pose a problem, but rather an opportunity for exciting planting.

There is no need for much bare soil to be seen. There are several suitable creeping or film-forming plants that can be used as ground cover, and *Selaginella*

The bird's nest fern, *Asplenium nidus*, is tolerant of a wide variety of conditions, but is not frost hardy. It is too big for the 'wardian case' treatment, but is a superb fern for the conservatory. Fairchild Tropical Garden, Coral Gables, Miami, Florida.
Nicola Kelly

kraussiana, a mat-forming, bright green plant, is one that will fit in perfectly with its close relatives, the ferns. However, it is with ferns themselves that you can cover the ground and also hide the bare stems of the plants that will grow and flower above them.

At the lowest level, *Adiantum capillus-veneris*, a British native maidenhair fern which is only hardy in the south and west, grows abundantly in the environment where it is safe from frosty winds, while *Davallia mariesii*, the hare's foot fern, and *D. trichomanoides*, which needs a 45 F minimum temperature, will provide delicate frond tracery of a different, more filigreed kind from the maidenhair.

On a larger scale the chain ferns, *Woodwardia* species, make superb conservatory plants, whereas they are a doubtful proposition outside. They are proliferous (which means that they make plantlets on their fronds) and thus good subjects for experimentation, but on the whole it is far better, once having obtained a specimen, to grow it in the shelter of the conservatory, while you

A small greenhouse devoted to ferns. King's Gatchell, Ottery St Mary, Devon.
John Kelly

try out some of its children in the open garden — so long as you live in a mild area or a city.

Woodwardia orientalis has three-foot fronds of fairly simple structure and is a most handsome plant, but if you want something really dramatic, *W. radicans* grows to six feet, with really bold, pinnate fronds, of which the individual lobes can be a foot long. Obviously it is not a plant for a small enclosure, but it is wonderful when over-topped by bright, tropical blooms and exotic foliage.

A much smaller fern, either for a confined space or perhaps as an echo of the big woodwardia, with which it shares some characteristics, is *Blechnum occidentale minor*, whose more simply pinnate fronds are only about a foot long. It is a fern that needs the warmer temperature in winter.

The conservatory is, of course, a good place in which to grow those ferns that are just on the margin of hardiness in your area, but which are justly regarded as belonging among the hardy ferns. The line to be drawn between hardy and tender is a very variable one that can change from garden to garden,

Polystichum polyblepharum growing in shade out of doors in Southern Ireland. Kells House, Co. Kerry, Ireland. *John Kelly*

let alone from one side of a country to another.

It is not necessary slavishly to follow pundits, writers of books and specialists in deciding what you will grow in the conservatory garden and what will be allowed to take its chance in the outside world. In Chapter 9 you will find several ferns, particularly varieties of *Polystichum setiferum*, that are perfectly hardy, and yet their finely-divided structures are so extreme that they are best appreciated and more likely to thrive under glass.

As we are considering ferns as garden plants, I think we have to think of the conservatory as an extension of the garden and not totally distinct from it. Just as the city gardener comes to realise that his environment is artificially enhanced and completely rewrites the concepts of hardiness, so can a gardener with a conservatory redefine hardiness within his own garden as a whole. This is why this is not a book exclusively about hardy ferns, but about ferns in the garden. A garden is, after all, an artificial environment *per se*.

This will all seem extremely elementary to a fern specialist, who probably has greenhouses devoted to tricky ferns, where filmy ferns lurk under bell jars and unbelievably rare tropical ferns steam gently.

Alternatively (or even also) he will have an alpine house, in which hardy ferns that hate winter wet, or ferns that are so small that the open garden would swallow them up, are kept in pots, plunged in a peat and sand mixture.

However, such places, although standing within the garden, are not of it. A well-planned and interestingly planted conservatory, on the other hand, can be or appear to be an integral part of the garden.

Partly this can be achieved by planting just outside the conservatory hardy analogues of plants inside. For example, if the scarlet passion flower, *Passiflora coccinea* were growing inside, the hardy *P. caerulea*, planted outside, would suggest an elision of the boundary between the glass structure and the outer environment. Similarly (and at the lower range of minimum winter temperatures) the abutilon 'Ashford Red' would be echoed by the smaller flowered but conspicuous *A. megapotamicum*, which only falls prey to winters in the coldest places.

However, it is not necessary to go to any great lengths along these lines. One such association would be quite enough for a conservatory which, on a summer's day, looked out even on such things as the humble petunia and nicotiana. After all, they are exotic enough, even though they may have come from a packet of seed from the supermarket.

It is inside that balance needs to be attained. So often one sees such plants as passifloras and abutilons putting on wonderful shows of spectacular colour and flower form higher up in the roof space, while their skinny trunks let the whole display down by their bareness. Here the combination of the essentially tropical air of ferns, their greenness, coolness, and great variety of restful and intriguing shapes and forms, can act as a perfect contrast to the heated tones of the flowers, and also disguise the deficiencies of plants made leggy by their enthusiasm for the light.

4

Woodland and Shady Gardens

It would be hard to find a natural woodland or forest anywhere in the world that did not have a population of ferns. Even boreal coniferous forest, where life is hard, winters unforgiving, and summers short-lived but torrid, supports ferns.

Their apogee is found in the wet, Tropical and Sub-Tropical forest. The teeming, steaming jungles of Malaysia are host to the largest fern fronds in the world, as well as a host of others, some of them most strange. Members of the extraordinary genus *Platycerium*, the stag's horn ferns, are found there, clinging to the branches of trees as they do right round the world, even on islands as botanically and geographically remote as the Seychelles.

The adaptability of ferns in the long term has been the source of their survival. The tropical ones have it all their own way. Ferns originally developed in a hot, humid world where their method of reproduction was ideally suited and they could grow mightily enough to become a major element in the formation of coal. As the earth's climate underwent wide changes, albeit over many millions of years, the ferns of the Tropical and Sub-Tropical regions would have felt little stress and not much need to change.

On the other hand, the Temperate regions, alternately swamped by mile-deep ice or flooded with shallow, lukewarm water; occasionally exposed to moderate, gentle climates, and latterly in places to persistent, gentle, leaching rain, provided Nature with a vast laboratory in which to test the ingenuity of her evolutionary process.

The ferns retained their love of high humidity and generous levels of free moisture, but learned that survival depended on these more than on the dense tree cover that ancestrally had provided them. Lakes and bowl-shaped depressions, bearing pine and sweet grass after the ice departed, slowly suc-

A legacy of the ancient world. *Ctenitis sloanii*, the Florida tree fern. Fairchild Tropical Garden, Coral Gables, Miami, Florida. *John Kelly*

cumbed to the nagging rain as their soils became podsolised* and as impervious to moisture as pudding basins. Peats, first those of fen vegetation, then those of bog mosses, filled the sumps and gradually became home to a unique type of flora, among which ferns thrived in the wet conditions with not a tree in sight.

Elsewhere, the ice scraped the rock bare, leaving only small crevices and pockets where a little soil could accumulate and give sanctuary to those ferns that could crouch down out of the wind and sun and get on with their family lives in the close moistness of the deeper cracks.

Meanwhile, where true Temperate woodland was developing, the going was easier, although far removed from the old days when millennia passed in the warm mists of dinosaur-time. The most sheltered nooks, the darker, moister banks, and the good, deep soils of oak and ash woodland with the annual bounty of leafmould, welcomed the survivors and allowed them to reproduce and found dynasties whose descendants we find in the woods and forests of today.

What this means for gardeners is that while woodland types of conditions are

* Podsols are soils whose mineral constituents have been leached over a prolonged period and have become concentrated in a layer through which water cannot pass.

the very best that can be offered to ferns, there are also ferns for completely different habitats. As we saw in an earlier chapter, the factors common to them all are vegetable soils rich in true humus, adequate to ample moisture, and protection from wind. The Victorian fernery was well over the top, founded as it was on assumptions about ferns that were by no means universally sound. Today's gardeners are in a position to understand ferns and, by understanding them, to use them in ornamentally exciting ways.

Woodland in the Garden

'Woodland' is a term that you come across a lot in gardening books. Without qualification it assumes much about society that is not true. We are not all blessed with tracts of trees; most of us have small gardens and the general trend is for them to get smaller.

However, qualified, it is a desirable term and the qualification opens up possibilities that people might hitherto have thought closed to them. Woodland need not be grand — it is nice if it is, of course — and can be achieved for all practical purposes in the sorts of gardens that today's housing developments allow.

It is really a matter of conditions, not of size. If woodland conditions can be created over a couple of square yards, the plants will not be aware that their home is that restricted. They can't edge over and have a look at the neighbours. They will thrive in their ignorance as well as if they were in the middle of Mr Badger's Wild Wood.

If you visit the garden of a real fern enthusiast, you will soon learn what 'woodland' means in a gardening context. A narrow border, backed by a tall hedge growing on a low bank, with another hedge or even a wall at right angles and perhaps a glasshouse standing in front of it, the whole only, say, three yards or metres by one, is a woodland as far as ferns are concerned. All it needs is for the soil to suit.

This is not a theoretical description, but an account of part of a Devon garden that I know well. The corner is not pretty, neither is it unattractive; it is a practical plot where the ferns are little short of perfectly accommodated. As far as they are concerned they are at the very edge of a dense wood (the hedge) and have as a neighbour the trunk of a mighty forest tree (the wall). The aspect is such that strong sunlight does not impinge upon them — the glasshouse absorbs most of that — and its lower storey provides positive shade, as do the plants and their pots inside on their staging.

If you would care to take a walk in a real wood — not one of those Surrey

Dryopteris filix-mas. Bramble Cottage, Ottery St Mary, Devon. *John Kelly*

commons where the beeches, grafted decades ago, stand like advertisements for elephantiasis, but a proper, unkempt, nettly, dock-strewn and bluebelled wood — I would ask you to look for where the greatest concentrations of young ferns and others of varying ages are to be found. It is certain that you will be drawn to the steepest but moistest banks, for those are the places where fern spores germinate with the greatest freedom.

If you were to drive down my *bohereen*, the little road that leads eventually to Killarney, you would see that the steep sides are thickly covered with ferns. At one place, royal fern (*Osmunda regalis*) predominates; at another shady spot, *Dryopteris dilatata* abounds. On rocks you will find mature clumps of *Asplenium trichomanes*, the maidenhair spleenwort; and hard fern, *Blechnum spicant*, is everywhere.

In a Devon lane you would see much the same sort of thing, but here the ferns may well be those adapted to drier places. Species of *Polypodium*, male and lady ferns are likely to abound. In Dorset, where it is drier still, *Polystichum setiferum*, the soft shield fern, often clothes the steeper lanesides.

The Devon garden, with its cunningly exploited hedgy corner which in other hands might have housed the compost heap, allows ferns from all these sorts of places to recognise the bank on which the hedge stands as the perfect germination site. All sorts of ferns come into being there, many of them with new kinds of frond formation; almost all of them interesting. Behind it all lies a lifetime's experience, a deep love of ferns, and much research. Beyond that, though, is an understanding of ferns, of what they need and, above all, why they need it.

Woodland on a grander scale does, of course, exist in gardens. Those who possess it are truly blessed so long as they are able to garden it well. Next door to the garden in Devon is another — so close that the owner uses a gap in their common hedge when visiting — in which ferns grow in a wood of heart-stopping beauty.

To illustrate the deep understanding of ferns that is evinced in this totally different place, I must digress and ask you to travel four thousand miles in a second or so, to the forests of Central Florida.

Not far from the Disney Corporation's version of Florida, a short distance from the urban amoeba that is Orlando, and a stone's throw from the seemingly endless mucklands, where vegetables grow on vast fields of billiard-table flatness, is the real Florida. This is not the Everglades — they are farther south— but the forest Florida that Poncé de Léon and the first Spanish explorers found.

The floor of the forest is swamp. It is not deep and some of it is not under water at all, but a gentle undulation of the land, only a foot or so between one place and another, provides squidgy, peaty, black ridges among the softly flowing seepages and the still pools that are divided into smaller ones by the roots of bald cypress and red maple.

There are ferns everywhere. Osmundas, including the American form of our own royal fern, stretch as far as the eye can see among the towering trees. The understorey of the forest is one huge mass of ferns, seedling magnolias, vines, and small shrubs on the drier tracts.

In the Devon woodland temperatures are, on average, thirty degrees Fahrenheit lower all the year round. And yet, if you take that mental journey back again, you will find yourself perfectly at home.

The squidginess and black peatiness are the same. The paths could as well have been made by generations of raccoons as by artifice (which in context makes you think of badgers), and the seepages amalgamate into wet, grassy saucers which in turn feed the slow-running trickle of a rill and its ponds.

Tall trees provide the canopy, but they are the ones you would expect in an English woodland. Nevertheless, the mixture of broad-leaved and coniferous trees is perfectly balanced for the provision both of adequate light and year-round shelter.

And, sure enough, ferns are everywhere, with *Osmunda regalis* stretching as far as the eye can see among the trees. There are dryopteris and blechnums and all sorts of others. It is a variation on an ancient theme, carried out by a modern gardener.

Such a triumph of emulation of Nature is only possible when she is understood, or if that is something too much for one lifetime to achieve, when she is treated with reverence and sympathy.

The world-wide kingdom of the ferns is further illustrated by the presence — in prefect harmony — of candelabra primulas and meconopsis from the Himalayas, *Gunnera manicata* from Brazil, *Lysichitum* species from eastern North America and from north-eastern Russia; almost every continent is represented. It is a garden that proves, if proof were needed, that ferns belong; they are the natural companions of flowering plants and do not belong merely in collections.

If you keep in mind the roles that ferns play in the wild, it will not matter if you only have a tiny area in which to grow them. You will still be able to set up your own version of the woodland environment. After all, the rock garden is regarded as one of the very best ways of gardening on a small scale, yet nobody would accuse you of *folie de grandeur* for claiming that you were successfully approximating to the conditions on a mountainside many square miles in area. A fern can take as much solace from a well planted Japanese maple only a few feet high as from a mighty oak.

However, having for some years presented gardening programmes on television, I have found that the best lessons for people with small gardens are to be found in large ones. It is much easier to scale down than to scale up and, besides, the lessons learned from small gardens are short, even though they may be profound. It is far easier for a producer to glean half an hour's worth of information-packed, entertaining material from a large garden with many aspects and nooks and crannies than it is to have to move his unit from location to location and patch it all together. Much cheaper, too.

Therefore, I would suggest that we look at a large model of a woodland garden and see what can be done with ferns in it. You can pick out the plums yourself for fitting into your own garden, whatever size it may be.

Ferns and their Woodland Associates

Our model woodland garden will not be homogeneous. It will have margins and a centre, drier and wetter places, areas of more sun than others, and parts where the soil is rich and deep, while elsewhere it may be poor and shallow.

The trees may be able to be hosts to ferns, and the mosses that grow on the northern sides of them (southern in my native New Zealand) and on banks and stones may have their own populations.

What ferns can we expect to see? That depends on the soil, but let us say in general that *Osmunda regalis, Blechnum spicant*, and *B. tabulare*, with *Matteuccia struthiopteris*, are likely to be found near or even in some cases in water. It is likely, too, that they will be among the ones that receive the most sun, for several reasons. One of these is that plants that have the most abundant supply of water can usually (but by no means always) tolerate the most sun. Another is that trees tend not to grow in water, with the result that the overhead canopy has a gap in it, which lets the sun in.

In the shadiest, most sheltered, and above all best drained places, and loving shady banks, we shall find *Dryopteris dilatata*, where it will form colonies with others, such as *Blechnum spicant* and the lady fern, *Athyrium filix-femina*.

The lady fern is tougher than her name suggests. She will grow in deep shade, in dripping wet places, or in spots that are a lot drier, but always where the drainage is good.

It is not so surprising, I suppose, that lady and male ferns should seek one another's company, even though it is merely their physique and not their sexual proclivities that determine their gender. Ferns are hermaphrodite (and that is an over-simplification!), and associate well across the genera, each intent on doing its own thing. In our woodland, different male ferns are likely to be in the company of the ladies, mostly on the drier, but not very dry, slightly elevated places.

In drier places still, but always short of drought, *Polystichum setiferum*, the soft shield fern, sets up its stall as the big toughie; the fern that can take anything . . . well, almost. The hard shield fern is actually less tough, despite its name. It is 'hard' because its fronds feel leathery; it needs more shade and shelter than its 'soft' cousin.

Where dryness can involve droughty periods, but still out of the strongest sun, and where opportunities can be indulged to the full (such as in the fork of an oak), the polypodies come into their own and provide that true touch of the Tropical. After all, no jungle or Sub-Tropical forest exists that has no epiphytes.

Of course, there are many more, and the numbers of varieties of the few species I have mentioned are enough to provide a life's work of study. However, even such a short list would enable you to create a truly ferny woodland garden on whatever scale you wished.

In what company are these different groups to be found? Naturally enough, among the plants that enjoy the same conditions. However, some of these are

Left: Fascinating shapes and feathery effects add magic to the woodland floor. Kells House, Co. Kerry, Ireland. *John Kelly*

Below: *Osmunda regalis* 'Crispa', *O.r.* 'Purpurascens' and *Osmunda regalis* in the background. In the foreground are *Dryopteris dilatata* 'Crispa Whiteside', *Dryopteris filix-mas* 'Polydactyla Crouchii' and *Matteuccia struthiopteris*, shaded by *Taxodium distichum*, the American swamp cypress. King's Gatchell, Ottery St Mary, Devon. *John Kelly*

more desirable than others, and it is the gardener's job — and, we hope, delight — to choose from among them the ones that will contribute to the very best, most balanced and harmonious of woodland gardens.

Early spring sees the laundry-whiteness of snowdrops demanding to be set against something green. If they are grown where the soil is bare, they will soon become dirty as the rain splashes soil all over them. A mossy spot, or one where last autumn's leaves have been wisely left to lie, is ideal, and an evergreen fern like *Asplenium scolopendrium* makes the perfect background.

This is my own favourite snowdrop-fern association. The cheerful glossiness of the hart's tongue's undivided fronds and the bright, white bells make a nonsense of the grimness of winter. Later, I enjoy the almost overstated, even vulgar display of polyanthus. Regal polyanthus, bred in Tasmania for enormous flowers, scent, frills, doubles, and all sorts of frivolities, are too much for some people. They are barmaids among plants but, true to that calling, they look perfect in the right context. Among the chewy-looking crispness of the hart's tongues, whose multiferous fronds provide a wealth of curls and flounces in fresh green, the polyanthus are at once appropriate and somehow toned down.

For all-year interest, a camellia will pick up the crispness and glossiness and translate it into another leaf shape and a vertical dimension. It will need acid soil, but will delight in the woodland conditions that the ferns enjoy. Pick a late-flowering one if it is coloured, or a pure, early white like *Camellia* x *williamsii* 'Francis Hanger', whose single flowers will complement the simpler polyanthus and will not clash with them.

The woodland shelter might partly be given by one of those variegated elaeagnus that are usually seen planted in precisely the worst possible places. There is no better use for them than to alleviate the themes of green and elongated shapes that are made by ferns. The short, ovate leaves do the same job as those of a camellia but, instead of echoing the texture of hart's tongue ferns, they introduce the sharp contrast of bright, golden yellow with their variegated leaves.

'Ferny' ferns, like *Dryopteris affinis, Athyrium filix-femina*, or any others with divided fronds, do not seem to work with either camellias or elaeagnus. You have to be very careful not to create a feeling of mere weediness. It is so tempting to think that the filigree of the lady fern or the Japanese painted fern will make a beautiful contrast with the glossy stiffness of a camellia, but the effect is one of neglect. With an elaeagnus it is similar, but the weedy impression that is made is even worse.

On the contrary, well-tended, well-spaced plants of the shuttlecock fern, *Matteuccia struthiopteris*, contrast brilliantly with either of these stiffly-habited shrubs. This is because it is a fern with an overall structure and outline that is missing in many others. You take in its ferniness, but you are impressed by its strongly built shape. It looks as though it was meant to be there. In woodland it is truly happy and can grow to be quite large — five feet in height is nothing special — although a three-foot matteuccia is more usual and impressive enough.

If your taste does not run to the more obvious charms of well-fleshed polyanthus, the well-brought-up daintiness of primroses may appeal to you more. They are not brash enough to compete with the dominating presence of male ferns like *Dryopteris affinis* that remain evergreen in mild districts, but they consort well enough with hart's tongues. In the drier woodland gardens where the soft shield fern likes to grow, primroses will flower while the old fronds are still green and will make them look less passé.

In late spring and early summer the taller Asiatic primulas come into their own. The candelabra primulas, whose two- to three-foot stems carry concentric whorls of flowers at well spaced intervals, are among the most lovely of all woodland plants. They can be grown in drifts of one colour or in broad masses in which the colour mixture, due to generations of hybridising among themselves, has been allowed full rein.

There are many plants among which candelabra primulas look happy. What is certain is that, like snowdrops, they greatly dislike bare soil. Their flat rosettes of leaves are too close to the ground for comfort when the soil is being splashed around by rain, and they soon feel the pinch when the strong sun of their flowering period draws the moisture from beneath them.

They need neighbours among which to raise their flower heads above cool, shaded roots. There are few better than ferns, and shafts of sunlight slanting down among trees, picking up the silver flash of an insect's wings as they highlight the stately colourfulness of the primulas, make fascinating patterns of light and shade among the fronds.

Primula pulverulenta is the most universally easy to grow, as it is permanent in gardens that are too hot and dry for many others. The sort of climate that is a primula paradise is something like that of Scotland, Ireland, or parts of the State of Washington, where temperatures are not too high in summer and where there is good summer rainfall (good for gardeners, that is). Its flowers are ruby-red and last for a long time, usually fading just as the bright, buttery yellow whorls of *P. bulleyana* take up the baton.

It is hard to think of any fern that is not a fitting companion for candelabra primulas. If the soil is acid and peaty, *Dryopteris dilatata* is perfect, its broad, much divided fronds benefiting from association with tall, upright stems and bright colours. Drier, loamier, more neutral to alkaline soils call for *Polystichum*

The broad buckler fern, *Dryopteris dilatata*, is widely distributed in the cooler parts of the Northern Hemisphere. Clodagh, Sherkin Island, Co. Cork, Ireland.
John Kelly

setiferum or *Asplenium scolopendrium*.

You can go wrong with candelabra primulas if you are not careful, as the colours are strong and clash easily. It is best to steer clear of the purple tones of *P. beesiana* and *P. burmanica*, and I have always tended to encourage yellow and pink.

P. pulverulenta 'Bartley Strain' is a shell pink form that comes partly true from seed. Once you have it, you can keep it going by division. Seedlings give a quicker increase, and sowing the seed is by no means to be frowned on. If seed is sown, however, only the largest gardens permit the growing of the normal red form as well, otherwise the strain will be hard to keep. All seedlings that turn out to have red flowers must be rogued out immediately. It is one of the most beautiful of all flowering plants, especially when seen in that slanting sunlight among trees, and if I were to find myself marooned at Ougoudugou amid sand and Bedou, it would be of these sumptuous but dainty pink candelabras, attended by cool ferns, that I would dream.

The Winter Woodland

Whether you are temporarily banished to an arid place (the Algarve, perhaps, or Lanzarote?) and have perverse longings for cool shade, or just wonder how to get the most out of a woodland planting, you will, as your planning goes on, begin to realise that the late winter and early spring are times when a large number of ferns are not much in evidence.

The reason for this is that they are deciduous. *Osmunda, Onoclea, Matteuccia, Athyrium, Cystopteris, Adiantum* and some *Dryopteris* species, to name a few, lose their fronds completely in winter. Others are evergreen — or are they?

The term 'evergreen' is a relative one. All plants lose their leaves; it is a matter of how often and how many. A truly deciduous plant loses its leaves all at once and loses all of them. Plants may be winter-deciduous or summer-deciduous, but most Cool Temperate and Cold Climate plants that behave like this lose their leaves in winter; summer leaf loss is an adaptation to drought.

In a way, so is the loss of leaves in winter. Frozen soil, combined with water loss from leaves (or fronds) leads to physiological drought. The roots cannot take up water to compensate for the loss of moisture to the atmosphere. Truly deciduous plants avoid this problem; evergreen ones have to cope with it as best as they can.

While all evergreens lose some of their leaves each year, usually in the summer, the mechanism involved is one of renewal, in which the new leaves detach the old as they emerge. A leaf may live for two, three, or more years, but eventually it becomes tired and old and of no great service to the plant and is discarded.

In winter, something else happens. A true evergreen will have devices at its disposal to stave off physiological drought. It may be, as with camellias, that the leaves have leathery outer layers that prevent desiccation. Perhaps a covering of hairs will have the same effect, as in the famed New Zealand vegetable sheep.* Rhododendrons roll up their leaves lengthwise so that they look like so many cheap cheroots hanging from the branches. No matter how ingenious their defences, though, a really severe winter will get through, unless they are real ironclads like the conifers of the boreal forests.

What happens then is that normally evergreen plants become defoliated, thus taking the strain off the roots. This in itself does no great harm; it is the stress on the plant during the following growing season, when it tries to renew all its leaves at once — a simple task for a deciduous subject — that weakens it. Two or three winters like that in a decade can be lethal.

Evergreen-ness in ferns is different. Generally speaking, the fronds last just a little over a year, becoming tired-looking in early spring and gradually fading

* As enthusiasts of alpines will know, these plants, which look like woolly grey cushions, are members of the genera *Raoulia* and *Haastia*. In the wild they may be several feet across, but in cultivation it is a triumph to grow one more than an inch wide.

Evergreen ferns in winter. Abbotsbury Gardens, Dorset. *John Kelly*

away after the new ones have arisen from the crown. Others last longer, but those who garden with ferns like to cut away the old fronds on such plants as *Polystichum setiferum* before the new fronds start to unfurl. This is simply garden tidiness as opposed to the way things happen in nature and is good practice, as no harm comes to the new fronds during the cutting-back process.

A large proportion of evergreen ferns may be looked on as being semi-evergreen in gardens. This is because they will retain their old fronds for more or less of the winter, depending on the severity of particular winters or upon the general climate in which they find themselves. After all, Japanese ferns, nearly all of which are evergreen, evolved in Japan, not in gardens in Nottingham, England, or Issaquah, Washington. Their adaptation to the threat of physiological drought is to relieve the strain on the roots by losing their fronds. Unlike other evergreen plants, however, this imposes no stress during the next growing season, as they are used to producing a full quota of fronds as a matter of course.

One way or another, then, you are going to have bare patches during the winter and spring where deciduous ferns grow, where you tidy up what we really should call semi-evergreens, and more so if you live in a chilly climate.

Bareness is anathema to gardeners. It looks dull and depressing and attracts every odd weed seed that is around – and in winter there are many more than you would think. Ferns, then, need companions even when they themselves are not in evidence.

Although it will vary a bit, the month of May is the one during which new fern fronds unfurl. There are exceptions, such as the polypodiums, which perform in summer, but in general May is when the garden is full of light, golden-green croziers.

So what of the bare areas before that? Obviously, it is a good idea to plant things that will flower before or just into May, but what? It is not much use thinking that pieris bushes, whose brilliant red new growths happen in April, will be any good. They are perfect companions for ferns in a woodland setting (or ferns are ideal for them), but not really as replacements in terms of garden interest. The same goes for early-flowering rhododendrons. Grow them with ferns by all means, but some other solutions must be found to fill the places where ferns were but are not now.

Bulbs spring immediately to mind and we have already thought of snowdrops. Glades and places where some sun filters through will support daffodils and narcissi if the soil is not sticky or badly drained (but then you wouldn't succeed with your ferns anyway, would you?). Early flowering daffodils are highly desirable, especially for growing quite close to the ferns. The one-foot tall 'Tête à Tête', for example, flowers in March, so when its leaves become overshadowed by the fern fronds in May, they will have done their work, as they need seven weeks from flowering for the bulbs to be adequately fed. 'February Gold' is just one of many others that can turn a fairly uninteresting woodland floor into a fascinating one.

Meanwhile, larger daffodils can accompany the evergreen ferns, particularly the strong growers like *Dryopteris affinis*, whose fronds are only removed by really hard frosts. What better partners are there for daffodils in a vase than cut fern fronds? It is a match that works just as ideally in the open garden.

In a small corner of our large model you are highly likely to find that an area where lady ferns grow – they are only two feet or so tall – has been colonised by *Cyclamen coum*. This is little more than two inches tall when in flower and has tough little blooms a bit like miniature ships' propellers in shades of pink, red, purple-red and white. Farther out, *Iris reticulata* is quite capable of flowering through a covering of snow, and if the soil is peaty, as it should be for lady ferns, the blue, cut-fringed fairy caps of *Soldanella villosa* will do the same if the snow is unseasonably late.

A quiet woodland pool, a ferny paradise. Bramble Cottage, Ottery St Mary, Devon.
John Kelly

Such an arrangement of winter interest — one which, in this case, makes you ascribe a bravery to the plants that they do not, after all, possess — is perfectly possible in the smallest garden. Indeed, there must be many a tiny city plot in which the daemon of the woodland can be conjured up in this sort of way. Once your imagination and plant knowledge get to work on this whole business of decorating the places where fern fronds are temporarily absent, your ideas will begin to evolve to a point where you actively relish using acute timing to produce dramatic effects.

It was Kenneth Adlam, of Ottery St Mary in Devon, who introduced me to the combination of lady ferns and *Meconopsis betonicifolia*, the Himalayan blue poppy. After donkey's years of growing *Athyrium filix-femina* and several of its varieties, and decades of familiarity with meconopsis, I was delighted to learn something new, and also a tiny bit piqued at not having had the idea myself.

The flowering time of the meconopsis coincides, except in years of warm springs following ultra-mild winters, with the unfurling of the fern fronds to the extent that it starts just before they begin and finishes as they attain their full length. So often one sees meconopsis flowering rather self-consciously alone or, much better of course, among the earlier asiatic primulas. It is only rarely that their full glory is displayed without distraction against a background of green, and it is a fine improvement on that to have created a dynamic combination in which the green background changes almost imperceptibly from day to day.

Waterside and Wet Places

In the wild, ferns love wetness, but it is almost always moving wetness. Stagnancy is the enemy of organisms that live on oxygen; movement allows water to dissolve oxygen and become a friendly environment.

Not that all that many ferns will grow actually in water, or with their feet in it. Perhaps the only hardy ones that will are the osmundas, and even they are better off for having their crowns out of the water itself.

Osmundas are astonishingly successful plants, growing wherever oxygenated boggy or swampy conditions are to be found. *O. regalis* occurs all over Europe and has managed to adapt to the West Indies, India, Uruguay, and a host of unlikely-seeming places. British fern-lovers consider it almost to have vanished from the wild of their ken; they would do well to forget their parochialism and visit south-western Ireland, where it is everywhere, a glory of the rocky, irregular countryside, romping in bogs, gallivanting on field boundaries, and slapping your car wetly as you drive along the lanes of Cork and Kerry.

It is a most elegant plant, with fronds five feet long or more in good, rich, moist conditions, in which it will take full sun if asked, but is generally better in dappled shade. The fronds are boldly and widely pinnate and of a tough texture, and arise from a mass of fibrous, peaty roots (osmunda fibre). They are quite different from those of other osmundas. The fronds that arise farther down are completely sterile, which is to say that they have 'normal' pinnae all the way up. Progressively higher fronds, which are also progressively close to the centre of the plant, are increasingly fertile, and are converted in part to bearing spores, the fertile parts looking rather like the flower heads of an astilbe after they have gone brown and set seed. The American species, *O. cinnamomea* and *O. claytoniana*, also have separate fertile fronds with some sterile pinnae.

As waterside decoration *O. regalis*, the royal fern, has few equals. It is a perfect foil for almost all the other plants that like similar conditions. In our large model woodland, in which we come upon a wet area with pools and trickles of water, the seven-foot tall *Gunnera manicata*, whose massive leaves may be as much wide, can be allowed to dominate. It is an eerie plant, ancient and primeval in appearance, with stems like those of a tropical bamboo, but unjointed and furnished with thorny, sharpened warts in a way that has led to their being likened to the workings of a Victorian musical box. Another analogy — again not mine and I can think of none better — has been applied to the leaves which, when rubbed gently, make a sound 'like a giant shaving'.

It has been likened to giant rhubarb, although it is related to no rhubarb at all. It is a jungle plant from southern Brazil, where it is not tropical, and it is the companion *par excellence* for the royal fern. The fern adopts a feminine grace against the overwhelming masculinity of the gunnera, but it is a fair-weather marriage only, as they both disappear in autumn, with only the pinkish resting cones, rather like huge cabbage-buds, left to be protected from the frosts.

The art of growing such large plants is to use their winter absence to your advantage. Strangely enough, and I have never become used to it, daffodils will grow strongly and flower reliably year after year if planted among the root masses of *Gunnera manicata*. And massive they are, too, with a well-developed root making a solid block of tissue about the size of a large armchair. But there again, the gunnera leaves do not develop fully until well into May, so the same thing applies as with growing bulbs where fern fronds will overshadow the soil later on.

However, there is more to it than that. When your happily married couple of gunnera and osmunda, with their acolytes that we shall shortly meet, have taken up their lowly winter stances, the clever gardener will allow the absence of their leaves and fronds to reveal a view, a feature, a group of plants, or some other surprise that could not be seen during the growing season. I have known this done so that a whole valley came into view that seemed not to be there in summer; in another garden the surprise was an entire pond, in yet another it was a stone figure.

Another contrast, involving a second, large, deciduous fern, is that between *Osmunda regalis* and *Matteuccia struthiopteris*, the shuttlecock fern. You are already familiar with the shuttlecock shape, which is in part due to its being the only hardy fern to make a stem. It is not a trunk like that of a tree fern, but a short, woody base from which the feathery, stiffly arching fronds arise. Its other sobriquet, 'ostrich feather fern', is appropriate and descriptive.

The two are entirely compatible both as to habitat and in terms of the way they look together. Add the gunnera and you could almost expect a long-lost dinosaur to come along looking for Momma. Ferns are great creators of atmosphere.

On a smaller scale, the sensitive, or American oak fern, *Onoclea sensibilis*, is ideal for wet places in gardens where osmundas and such giants as gunnera are too large. It is a little invasive, but is easily controlled, and its delightful

Onoclea sensibilis on the woodland floor. Keukenhof, Lisse, Holland. *John Kelly*

fronds, which are pinnate, each pinna looking more like the leaf of a Hungarian oak than an American one, arise individually from a rhizomatous rootstock and are branched. Like the other lovers of wetness, it can be grown in a good, rich, vegetable soil that stays moist throughout the summer. It is deciduous, and works very well in a long-term planting with small, early daffodils like 'Tête à Tête', 'February Gold', 'Jumblie', and 'Minnow'. Dividing either fern or the clumps of daffodils will do no harm to the planting as a whole.

Ferns that run are no problem; with the exception of bracken they can be removed with ease from where they are not wanted, and the plants so detached are always welcomed by friends or the plant stall at the local garden society. Bracken can creep in before you know it, though, especially in moist, rich places.

A warning about bracken has to be sounded at some time, so it might as well be now. It is one of the most invasive plants on earth, each individual being entirely capable of covering several acres. It can arise from bad samples of peat or from spores, and the better the conditions you have created for ferns, the more you need to keep an eye out for it. *Pteridium aquilinum*, the common bracken, is, so Reginald Kaye tells us, 'very difficult to transplant successfully'. I'm glad he tried rather than I, but it is interesting that a plant that is so fiendishly difficult to eradicate will not move happily. The uninitiated might at first sight take young bracken for a lady fern, but that illusion is soon dispelled when you appreciate that only the bracken has branched, individual fronds arising from a ferociously wandering rootstock.

Bracken is highly carcinogenic and has recently been recognised as a possible major cause of lung and other cancers. Its production of sharp needles of silica make it a menace to livestock, and it is generally bad news. Those who have gathered browned bracken in the past for horse-bedding or, perhaps more close to home, those who have used it to keep the frost from tender or young plants, had better stop now, for their health's sake. The inhalation of spores from autumn bracken is to be avoided at all costs.

If you find your garden has some bracken in it, don't panic. If you assiduously pull every frond straight upwards, it will come up with a few inches of black, underground stem. Keep doing this and you will be brackenless in about three years. Use gloves.

Two species of *Thelypteris* are lovers of moisture. They are haters of lime, though, so not everyone can grow them. *T. palustris*, the marsh fern, is a wanderer, but is entirely suitable for the smaller waterside garden. It is not as impressive as *T. limbosperma*, the mountain fern, which is notable for the delightful citrous scent of its fronds when you brush by them — its other name is lemon-scented fern. This is, according to some authorities, *Oreopteris limbosperma*. In its time it has also been *Thelypteris oreopteris, Dryopteris oreopteris*, and *Lastrea montana*. The marsh fern, according to some botanists, is *Thelypteris thelypteroides* subsp. *glabra*. It has in its time been *Dryopteris palustris, Dryopteris thelopteris* and *Lastrea thelypteris*. While one bends over backwards in one's attempts to empathise with botanists and their advances in the science of taxonomy, sometimes one wishes they would get their confounded act together.

In general it can be said that a garden without ferns is missing something, but it can still be a perfectly superb garden. On the other hand, a woodsy, leafy, squidgily moist garden with watery pools and seepages, whether naturally occurring or manufactured, is diminished by the absence of ferns.

Indeed, as a broadly-based gardener who is not one of the single-minded devotees of ferns (there are few; most fern lovers delight in plants as a whole), I have to say that such a garden is incomplete unless it is, if not dominated by ferns, then at least highly populated by them. It is my personal view that species, uncomplicated by the more advanced variations that occur — cresting, divisilobe, plumose, and so on — are the most appropriate ferns for such places, even if they are very small. The others are more appropriately grown in beds of ferns on their own or in borders that are a little more formally gardened.

Polypodium vulgare 'Cornubiense'. King's Gatchell, Ottery St Mary, Devon. *John Kelly*

5

Ferns in the Rock Garden

ALTHOUGH WE look back on the Victorian ferneries with a certain air of superiority, we would do well not to be too patronising. The people who made them were observant; with the scientific knowledge we have now, one suspects that they might, with their disciplined minds, have put us a little to shame.

Their use of rocks among and between which to grow ferns was based on observations in nature. However, it was the steep bank, dripping with drainage water from above, or the alga-glazed side of a chasm, glittering with rivulets, that inspired them. The more open, sunny rocks were hardly represented at all.

Modern gardeners who have been alerted to the value of ferns as garden plants, as opposed to items in collections, have benefited from the great advances in rock gardening that have taken place since the turn of the century. Then, it was *de rigueur* to outdo your neighbour at constructing mini-Matterhorns, sometimes complete with manikin Whympers, accoutred with knickerbockers and ropes. As a small boy, I helped to pull weeds from a monstrous pyramid, set with glaring white rock, that supported a dreadful, equally white stone planter, in which I seem to remember geriatric plants of no immediate provenance that begged release from their shame. It was a relic of a bygone age; a horticultural dinosaur that nevertheless worked its way into my blood and insidiously instilled a love of rock gardening that has never left me.

I have, however, had the good fortune to live in an era during which the art and craft of rock gardening has come of age. It has been plant-led, with the desires of the plants causing growers to look hard at the immediate environments of the plants and not at the irrelevant larger scene.

Gradually, the old favourites, such as dwarf phlox, aubrieta, the smaller dianthus and alpine penstemons, took over from great swaths of snow-in-summer, out of scale daffodils, and wallflowers. They were joined by plants

Athyrium filix-femina and the heather-like foliage of *Grevillea sulphurea*. Kells House, Co. Kerry, Ireland. *John Kelly*

which had hitherto been regarded as tricky, as the ideals of rich but very gritty soils, crevice planting, the placing of rocks so as to provide varied aspects, and a cool, deep root run were realised. At the present time it is possible to grow in the open plants that not so long ago were regarded as impossible except in an alpine house or frame.

Among the alpine enthusiasts there has always been a select band of those whose chief joy was to grow ferns in the rock garden. Among them in turn has grown a number of gardeners for whom the most natural thing in the world is to include the appropriate ferns among the other plants that properly belong among rocks, screes, crevices and stony pockets. However, some of the most eminent writers on ferns still tend to consign them to the shady side of the rock garden or to a rock garden constructed in shade. There is some room for a little direct thinking on the subject of shade; if it is applied, some interesting and useful factors emerge that will help us in deciding how to grow many of our ferns.

There are three kinds of shade; full, part (which itself is of two kinds), and equivalent.

Full shade is that which is found either in north-facing places or those that are overlooked by large rocks or buildings. It can also be a result of too dense an overhead canopy of leaves. Part shade is either created by the sun's movement causing a plant to be in sun for part of the day only, or takes the form of dappling under deciduous trees. Equivalent shade is a concept evolving from the sun's strength in high latitudes.

In full shade, sunlight reaches the plants, but sunshine does not. If it is caused by rocks or buildings it is usually a damp environment, but if trees are preventing rain from reaching the soil, dry shade results — the nightmare of gardeners everywhere.

Part shade created by the sun's movement causes plants to be in full sun for that part of the day when they are not in shade. Simple. However, there is no such thing in gardening as 'part sun', and a similarly arbitrary piece of logic dictates that a plant is in full sun unless it is in shade for a *significant* part of the day. For example, writers on the subject of cushion saxifrages usually advise that they be grown in full sun but where they receive some shade at the hottest part of the day.

Equivalent shade is a term of my own coinage. It is not the result of an attempt to appear academic, but seems to me to be a handy and fairly exact term for the phenomenon which allows plants that burn up in full sun in Surrey to thrive in it in Perthshire. It also causes *Camellia japonica*, which flowers wonderfully in full shade in the south of England, to demand full sun if it is to bloom in Northumbria. In Perthshire it will not flower at all.

The weaker sun in the higher latitudes of Scotland permits 'shade lovers' like petiolarid primulas to grow without shade. Thus there is a scale of sun strength that corresponds to a scale of degree of shade. I do not intend to formalise it mathematically, chiefly because mathematics and I have enjoyed a vendetta all my life, during which my opponent's victory has been absolute. I would merely ask that gardeners be aware of where they live in relation to latitude.

Other climatic factors are significant, too. Low rainfall areas, such as East Anglia, where twenty inches a year is not uncommon, are not inimical to ferns, but they make fern culture just a little more tricky than in West Cork or Cumbria, where one hundred inches falls without undue comment. Not only does the dampness of high rainfall suit ferns thoroughly; it follows that the more it rains, the less the sun shines and the more shade there is *per diem*. It goes without saying more than we already have that winds and ferns are not a good combination, and heat, as opposed to sunshine, is not the best thing for them, either.

As a very rough guide, you can take it that most ferns should be grown facing

Asplenium billotii, a small spleenwort that is a rare inhabitant of cliffs near European and Atlantic island coasts. Ilnacullin, Garinish Island, Co. Cork, Ireland. *John Kelly*

north in the south. North of Edinburgh they can almost all face south. In between, you will have to use your judgement. I have always trusted my judgement, which has usually consisted of snooping around other people's gardens to see what succeeds with them.

It is not necessary, then, to make specially shady rock gardens for ferns. With any well-constructed rock garden there will be shaded pockets, crevices, and cool rock faces – otherwise it would be unbalanced, and such things as ramondas, haberleas, ourisias and omphalodes would not have anywhere to live.

Furthermore, places with cool root runs under rocks will be perfectly capable of supporting ferns that receive the sort of part shade created by the sun's movement. They may even allow quite delicate ferns to be in full sun, especially where there is a high equivalent shade factor.

The two maidenhair ferns that are reliably hardy in the British Isles, *Adiantum pedatum* and *A. venustum*, respond remarkably well to this treatment. Both grow from rhizomes that must not be much more than half an inch below soil level, and both require peaty soils. At first sight they are not easy to accommodate in a sunny situation, as their roots would soon become burnt up and their soil rendered hot and dusty. However, three gardens spring immediately to mind in which maidenhair ferns have been perfectly happy in more or less sunny situations. In Hampshire *A. pedatum* was glossily green in full sun, its roots tucked among small rocks on a broad, hot scree. In Devon it grows similarly wandering among stones, but with a little shade for part of the day, and in Herefordshire the two species intermingled in a trough. The trough was divided in two by a wall, or perhaps there was a trough on each side of the wall — no matter. What was significant was that the trough on the more shady side received the equivalent, I suppose, of half a day's sun, and the roots, while topdressed with shingle, did not appear to need the cooler run provided elsewhere by larger stones.

It is worth noting that Hampshire and Devon are in the south of England, while Herefordshire is a county of moderate rainfall.

In my own garden, lady ferns tucked under the lowest tier of a rock bank that faces south-east are in sun from early morning to late afternoon in summer (the mountains get in the way of the lower sun of winter) and are as lush and green as you could wish. Of course, the rainfall is high and the soil is peaty, but the illustration reinforces the point that ferns can be excellent rock garden plants in their own right without being cast into the nether darkness.

Of course, the dictum that a rock plant is one that looks 'right' in a rock garden is as good a definition as you will get. Nobody these days insists on restricting rock garden plants to those that are botanically alpines. This goes for ferns, too, and a rock garden fern is one that looks 'right' in a rock garden. You may well ask who is to be the judge of rightness. The answer is you. It is your garden.

Earlier, I mentioned that ferns from other countries mutate, especially in Britain, into forms that are unknown in their native countries. British ferns with strange and beautiful changes in their structures can be found in the wild and in cultivation. Changes that involve reduction in size often lead to plants that are eminently suitable for the rock garden, and these plants, along with the naturally saxatile ferns, constitute the menu from which rock gardeners or fern fans can choose.

Given the need for cool root runs, and given the sorts of nooks and crannies in which ferns on rock are found in nature, crevice planting is an ideal way of introducing ferns to the rock garden. However, it is very difficult to do properly after the rocks have been put in position, and it is a good thing to plant as many of your ferns as you can as the rock garden is being built.

The account of how to build a rock garden has been done to death and with little eye towards the modern world. Rock is fiendishly expensive. When it was cheap, it was all very well to talk of ordering lorry loads (plural) and to intimate that labour (also plural) might be found on every street corner just dying to earn a few bob 'for a pint'. Rocks of enormous size were to be 'moved' into position and then at least two thirds of their bulk buried in the soil!

Nowadays people like to see what they have paid for, especially with rock at the price it is. Burying more than a little of it is out of the question. Anyway, smaller rocks can be manoeuvred by most of us with a little help from the family now and then. What is more, crevice planting is thus made far easier.

What you do is to choose two rocks, each of which has a face that matches the other; put them together and they might have been one rock – almost. You place the first one, and now at last do what the books tell you, which is to ram the soil beneath and behind it so that it does not move when stood upon.

You then take your fern from the bucket in which its root ball (out of its pot) has been soaking. It will have lost quite a lot of soil to the water and you will be able to squeeze the root ball with the minimum of damage. Choose a spot on the face of the first rock where the approach of the second will leave a small gap between them, lay your fern against it, and ram the second rock against the first.

Holding the second rock in position, ram its soil in turn beneath and behind it until it is solidly positioned. Now, taking a small amount of soil at a time, shove, tease, insinuate and wangle soil into the crevice in which the fern is sitting, crown level with the newly created (riven) rock face, until you are satisfied that the fern's roots are happily esconced in a snugly fitting, but not too compacted, home.

The soil, if it is peaty enough or made of well-rotted leaf mould, will remain in good heart no matter how strongly you use your braced finger-tips, karate style. It it is too loamy it will puttify, so prepare it beforehand. All this talk of muted violence might lead you to suppose that the plants will be damaged. Don't worry. The more experience a gardener has, the more he knows that he can go a long way in apparently physically mistreating plants; whereas he has far less latitude in matters of water, oxygen, light and temperature.

Imagine trying to plant a fern in such a small crack once the rock garden is made. Well, of course you could, but it would not be a nursery specimen. Later, after you have learned to propagate ferns (from this book, naturally), you will be able to take small sporelings or divisions and introduce them to quite minute crevices. For now, though, you will be wanting to make an immediate effect

A chance, crested sporeling of *Dryopteris filix-mas*. Kells House, Co. Kerry, Ireland.
Nicola Kelly

and to sample the richness that fern fronds give to the rock garden — hardly a place where foliage is usually the main attraction.

In full sun and in just such little cracks, some of the ferns that are naturally small and which favour analogous positions in nature are ideal. *Asplenium trichomanes*, the maidenhair spleenwort of my stable walls, is perfect. It will grow in shade, too, where it will tolerate dryness, but in sun it likes the coolness and moisture that is found behind and between the rocks.

You will often find it in nature in crevices above ledges. On the ledges, the devil's bit scabious is quite likely to raise its blue powder puffs eight to ten inches to the level of the fern's fronds. You won't see it in limy areas, but it does not matter; a globularia from the shady edges of white limestone screes in the eastern Alps will occupy the same rock garden crevice and produce an effect, with its two-inch stems end equally blue buttons, that is neater and, if anything, better.

This question of lime is a tricky one at first, but fairly simple in the end. Lime-hating plants will not grow where the soil is charged with calcium carbonate or other chemicals that fall under the label 'calcareous' (*cailc*, pronounced between 'kalk' and 'kaulk', is Irish for chalk — and was before the Romans adapted the word from Gaulish). Plants that tolerate or even like lime are almost certain to be unaffected by its absence. There are few acid-haters, although some plants, such as dianthus, may be shorter lived in moderately acid conditions.

Asplenium ceterach, the rusty-back fern, is said to prefer to have some old mortar rubble mixed with its soil. This could well be so, as I have only known it in old walls, in limestone rock gardens, or in a pot with limestone chippings as a top dressing. One day I must experiment with it in a more acid environment. Meanwhile, why not follow the herd and give it the mortar? The acquisitive instincts of a determined gardener know no bounds, but do restrict yourself to legality; farmers whose barns fall down under the assault of massed herds of ravening fern growers are apt to shoot first and ask questions later. Anyway, you only need a small handful, if that.

It is a pretty little fern, fairly unusual in having distinctly alternate pinnae. These are undivided and have silvery undersides that become rusty brown with age. It is the original spleenwort in the sense that it was used centuries ago as a nostrum for disorders of the spleen, but such things owed more to belief than science and you will not find it mentioned in modern herbals.

The common polypody,, *Polypodium vulgare*, and its close relative, *P. australe*, are remarkable in their toleration of drought (remember the smithy roof?). They are capable, especially the former, whose fronds are narrower, of colonising rocky places in dry shade and will often show a preference for them over moister corners. In a garden in the middle of the town of Wells, in Somerset, a classic bad dream of dry shade — a dusty corner beneath overlapping beech branches, raised above ground level and in the shadow of a wall to boot — sported but one plant that was surviving; a weary but obstinate polypody. The rest of the garden, I hasten to add, was excellent in every way.

If the polypodies are given better conditions — stony but leafy, and not too moist — they will spread and make ground-covering colonies in the most civilised manner. An annual mulch of well-rotted leaf mould is the ideal. If you are in a city and find it hard to obtain, take a sack along to your local park in the autumn and ask if you can have some fallen leaves. Choose oak if you can, or beech, but avoid evergreen oak. Do this each year, but allow the first year's leaves to rot for two years. You want to attain the consistency of compressed, well-molassed tobacco at the very least. Really good leaf mould is like coarse, black flour. Be tactful; parks staff take it amiss when people draw up in Swedish estate cars and proceed to unload sheaves of sack bags done up with string. It is better to ask first with an air of gentle diffidence. *Then* you can raid the place.

The three British polypodies (the third is *P. interjectum*) have provided us

with a large number of varieties. The polypody frond is, strictly speaking, pinnatifid. This is different from pinnate in that the fronds are divided almost to the midribs, but not quite. Pinnate fronds are completely divided. The divisions are still called pinnae, though. In some varieties the pinnae are split-ended like fingers, crested, or themselves pinnate, and they may be more or less narrow, broad, blunt or pointed.

The effects of what sound like terms from pathology are often most beautiful, and the crispness and greenness of these small ferns is something greatly to be sought after for the rock garden. What is more, the fronds are retained throughout the winter, and it is not until June or July that they wither away as the new ones are formed. They are a delight with rock plants like the soft pink – *Geranium dalmaticum*, which revels in the same stony conditions and has much the same propensity for gently colonising by means of its creeping rhizomes. The white form, too, is good. The art is to keep close associates of the ferns to plants that look as though they belong. By this I mean that *Geranium sanguineum lancastriense*, which again is a pleasant pink, sits well with polypodies, but *G.* 'Ballerina', whose flowers are purple-pink, veined with deep purple, is too much for them.

Nothing rampant or likely to climb all over the ferns should be allowed near them. Their fronds can mix with the leaves of low-growing plants, which is why I have cited geraniums, whose neatly cut leaves are perfect foils for the fern, but trailing brooms, *Phlox subulata*, and other robust mat-formers are bad companions for them, even though they much enjoy the same conditions.

One of the problems that have to be faced by those who would like to grow a wide variety of species, as opposed to many different forms of a few species, is that nurseries, even those that are the most specialised, cannot stock everything. Some of the species they do stock are sometimes represented by enough plants only for them to offer a few every couple of years or so. However, to fail to recommend plants merely because they are not too easy to come by is to dodge the column. If you are sufficiently encouraged to look for the rare and the beautiful, you will find it one day, either in commerce or among friends.

Such a fern is the limestone polypody, which is not a *Polypodium* species, but *Gymnocarpium robertianum*. Its fronds are anything from six inches to nearly two feet in length, and it likes nothing better than to weave its way deep among limestone rocks the size of one's shoes. The dark green fronds are a bit like the oak fern.

The oak fern itself is very adaptable, and loves to run about in gravelly but richly leafy soil. It is a good one to grow in a wider, shadier pocket in the rock garden, but not if you are hard up for space. This is *Gymnocarpium dryopteris*,

Polypodium interjectum growing wild close to the Atlantic Ocean. Sherkin Island, Co. Cork, Ireland. *Nicola Kelly*

Phegopteris connectilis (beech fern), with *Gymnocarpium dryopteris* (oak fern) behind. King's Gatchell, Ottery St Mary, Devon. *John Kelly*

and is a British native. It is one of the most ravishing of all ferns, a lover of limestone, and one to be hunted down at all costs. It must not be confused with the American oak fern, *Onoclea sensibilis*, which is not above ground for nearly so long, as its fronds are sensitive even to the slightest frost.

The American plant likes different conditions and needs the space of a larger rock garden. In the Keukenhof, in Lisse, near Amsterdam, where the bulb growers make their magnificent spring display, it emerges as the earlier daffodils of the shadier corners finish. At the feet of a large, domed rhododendron bush is a yard-wide stretch of soil between it and a lawn. Here small woodland daffodils make a bright ribbon in March, to be succeeded by the foot-high canopy of oak-like leaves for the rest of the growing season. In a shady pocket in a large rock garden, just such a succession would work beautifully. After all, to imitate sincerely is warmer than flattery, and the Dutch have much to teach us.

In contrast to the oak fern (British Isles version), which loves to grow on limestone formations, *Cryptogramma crispa*, the parsley fern, is a fanatical lime hater. It is a real treasure for a granite crevice in dappled shade and a leafy soil. Peat seems to be too wet for it, and a gravelly, moist leafmould mixture is best. It looks just like the unpinched sort of parsley; the fronds that are simpler in structure are the fertile ones and, at about a foot long, are usually four or five inches longer.

The principles involved in growing ferns in walls are much the same as with rock gardens. It all depends what you mean by a wall. It is very difficult indeed to induce *Asplenium trichomanes* to grow in minute cracks in the tightly-built stone wall of a building; you really have to wait for a spore to find itself a happy home. It is no good throwing spores at the wall either, as you can with seeds of campanulas, *Erinus alpinus*, or *Aethionema grandiflora*. Mind you, I have seen the fern growing in the company of just those plants when they had been artificially sown, but it has just 'happened'. As you will see, fern spores are a different matter from seeds.

However, a wall that is constructed specifically as a place for plants to grow, as well as for fulfilling a structural role in the garden, is a different matter, and great fun can be had by furnishing it with a population of ferns.

Making Wall and Peat Wall Gardens

If your garden is tiny and flat, you might as well skip the next few pages, unless you want to carry on merely for the sake of the entertainment. On the other hand, you may have the sorts of ambitions that make you wish that you had a bigger place with more possibilities. I believe these are nowadays called aspirations.

The very first garden that I was entitled to call my own was in the north-east of England. It was small and lay behind my three-bedroomed semi-detached. Limited though it was, I decided to divide it up into a vegetable garden and an ornamental garden with a lawn. In fact, there were two lawns, as I did not fancy breaking up the concrete path that divided them.

I divided it by building a low, double retaining wall. I wish I had grown some ferns on and in it, but in those days I was falling in love with alpines in a big way and did not give them a thought. However, I could have done so and now find myself endeavouring to steer your aspirations in the direction of building walls in which to grow alpines *and* ferns.

When I look around and see the countless gardens in which divisions of space are made with sterile structures built of concrete or reconstituted stone, I marvel at the income that is disposable on such things. They are often most tastefully done; sometimes with the aesthetic sense of a cave bat, but however executed,

Asplenium trichomanes, the maidenhair spleenwort, growing in a flight of stone steps. Ilnacullin, Garinish Island, Co. Cork, Ireland. *John Kelly*

they can never be home for more than the odd clematis, self-consciously trying out the pseudo-Florentine latticework while tentatively pushing at the putatively Roman tiles.

Having remarked on the cost of rock as compared with days gone by, it seems inconsistent to recommend that money made available for masonry partitions be earmarked instead for good, honest stones. *Tant pis*. The subject is ferns and their comfort, not economics.

There are three kinds of walls that are ideal for the purpose. The first is the single retaining wall, which is a structure born as often out of necessity as out of horticulture. A steep bank that might slip, slide, or otherwise collapse, and which in any case would be a repository for weeds and difficult to cope with, is faced with stone, built upwards in courses as if with bricks.

You will often see this kind of wall where house drives lead between curved banks at the splayed end, and all those grassy Devon banks containing lanes that are never quite wide enough for two cars to pass are made in a similar way, as you will soon find out if you collide with one.

The second kind is the double retaining wall, which is in effect a dry stone wall with a central core of soil. It can be made almost as wide as you like and, in turn, it is like the Irish bank, onto whose top knowledgeable horses put their feet when clearing it.

The third is really a specifically ornamental version of the second, made so that it has waves, embayments, embellishments and differing levels of flat areas instead of just one.

They are all magnificent homes for ferns, particularly the last, as it can be made to have almost whatever proportion of sun and shade you wish.

It is most important that the structure should be able to stand almost indefinitely. Nothing is more embarrassing than to find that a week of rain has turned your fine wall into something resembling a *steinschlag* on a Swiss mountain road. You achieve stability by using key stones – long ones driven into the bank or laid in, in the case of double walls — frequently at lower levels where the strains are greater and progressively less so as you work upwards.

Drainage is just as important in a wall as elsewhere. Just because a site is elevated does not mean that it is well drained. Think of high mountain bogs or the water cylinder in the loft. Surprisingly often I am approached by bewildered gardeners whose plants fail from rotted roots when planted in steep walls. What has almost always happened has been that they have used unadulterated garden soil.

The mixture that will best benefit ferns will also be the most welcome for alpines, whether shade- or sun-loving. It is fatuous to give ratios and proportions; all the best gardeners that I know just throw their composts together, but the general guideline is to make it as 'leafy' as possible and gritty enough so that when you squeeze a handful near your ear you can hear it crunching like sugar.

'Leafy' means 'well-rotted vegetable matter'. A head gardener I know composts hundreds of bales of wheat straw every year, but then he has the room. If you can, it is a good idea to let some rot down, but you need at least a dozen bales to make it worth while. However, such an amount, mixed with the products of your excursions to the parks department for leaves and any good stuff from the riding school's heap, and added to about one third of its bulk of *good* garden soil (never, never clay) will be just the job for filling your wall.

If you use the third kind of wall, you need not waste your good compost on all of it but fill in with rubble where you do not want plants to grow — where you make a stone seat, for instance.

The great secret, as with making a rock garden, is to plant as you go. It is even more important in wall planting, as you are using crevices to a very large extent, and trying to remove a stone at a later date in order to fit in a plant can be like pulling out the bottom can in a hill of beans.

You can use horizontal crevices to good advantage in wall building. They are easy to manage, as you simply lay the plant on the rock and the soil behind before laying the next stone on top. The great thing is to have the plant sloping downwards into the mass of the wall.

All planted walls should be built with a slope inward from base to apex and with each stone sloping inward and downward. This prevents burst due to rainwater, as the effect of gravity on the wall will be to bind it together. Furthermore, rain will go into the wall and thus the soil, making that cool root run that ferns love so much. If this is not done, tough rock plants may survive perfectly well, but you will not succeed with ferns.

A successful, shady wall will eventually become as good a place for ferns as a bank in a wood. You will certainly find odd sporelings in the dry, sunny part. As a matter of fact, as I write I am slightly distracted by having just found one on my own sunny wall that I am at a loss to identify. All the clues are there, but they fail to add up.

However, it is much better to let your ferns grow in company, and it is as bad a gardening practice to let them take over as it is with anything else. A deliciously placed and well made wall that has, for instance, been totally colonised by the regular forms of *Athyrium filix-femina*, is a waste. It would be much better occupied by a mixture of ferns and other plants.

Haberleas, ramondas and hepaticas are ideal, but then so are many other plants. Dwarf cyclamen and narcissi of the bulbocodium persuasion look wonderful in the shady pockets of the type three wall; Reginald Kaye always had massive corms of *C. hederifolium* tucked into the most unlikely corners of his walls among the ferns, and I believe that anything he has done in gardening is good enough for me.

Not all ferns like peat, but then most peat lovers enjoy leafy soils without peat. It is a waste of space and inappropriate to grow heathers in a wall, but some heather relatives are properly at home in them.

Of course, you can make your walls from peat blocks. You can buy fuel blocks readily, but they must be soaked in water for a few days before they are used. Do not build them higher than three feet at most, otherwise collapse will occur in about three years. The main drawback with peat walls backed by peaty soil is that they are almost too good, and you will find them to be the ideal germination site for wild ferns.

I had peat walls for many years in different gardens and loved them dearly. It is not a good thing to be too facile in recommending them, as the peat is not

Asplenium adiantum-nigrum on the Cork/Kerry border, Ireland. *Nicola Kelly*

always easy to obtain and the technique of building is fairly exact. However, as long as you put your peat wall garden in the shade (drying out is a big danger, especially in times of hosepipe bans) and weed it regularly, it is great fun.

The main weeds will be ferns. This will be because you will be growing them on it and elsewhere and the numbers of spores that will fall will be astronomical. You will have to be ruthless and grub them out, thrusting fingertips under the little crowns and tweaking them out. If anything really interesting turns up, keep it, of course.

Here the companion plants will be phyllodoces, trilliums, the smaller candelabra primulas like *P. cockburniana*, the better-behaved gaultherias, *Bruckenthalia spiculifolia*, andromedas, *Kalmiopsis leachiana*, cassiopes, erythroniums, and a host of gardening's most mouth-watering jewels, including the incomparable Asiatic gentians of autumn but excluding heathers, whose rightful place is elsewhere.

They in their turn will be enlivened, refreshed and enhanced by the ferns, whose delicate, lacy beauty will provide foliage on a different, more generous scale than the hummocks, cushions and threading, prostrate stems that are so typical of peat garden plants.

When building with peat blocks, the same principles of construction apply as for stone walls. They are regular in size, so lay them like bricks but, unlike a bricklayer, set each course just a little back — about half an inch — from the front of the one below. You will also let them slope downwards and into the wall, thus allowing the rain and your irrigation to be collected and not rejected.

Your mortar will be a very peaty soil, again just gritty enough to sound like sugar, and you will do the whole ramming business just as you would with a rock garden. Gaps and air pockets are asking for slugs and mice to make their homes in them, and you will not have much of a garden if you encourage either.

Some ferns will not like the peatiness, but if you stick to those listed on p. 103 you need not worry about that. The great thing about the rock garden, wall, and peat wall environments is that they are ideal for showing off and enjoying the smaller ferns that would otherwise be lost in the general hurly-burly of the mixed border. For this reason they are good homes for some of the more dainty of the mutated forms of species, and it is here that we must divert from the garden and enter briefly the world of the structure of ferns, otherwise I cannot use the terms of description that now become essential. A full list of ferns suitable for rock and wall gardens will be found at the end of the next chapter.

6

Fern Shapes and Changes

WHEREAS THE whole purpose of this book is to persuade you that ferns are garden plants in their own right, and to encourage you to grow them without the diffidence that is attendant upon dealing with something 'different' or 'specialised', I have to say that ferns are in many ways entirely different from the vast majority of other plants with which we are normally familiar.

Leaving aside the mechanism of their reproduction (we shall return to it when the subject of propagation is imminent), a fern's reproductive processes determine its difference from the flowering plants.

Flowering plants bear seeds, which are contained in special vessels — pods, fruits, and so on — and which develop on special growths arising from the stems. Ferns have no seeds, but bear spores, and these are carried on the part of the plant that is analogous with a leaf.

I say 'analogous', because every above-ground part of a fern is an analogue of its counterpart (where it has one) in a flowering plant. Ferns do not have leaves; they do not flower, the word 'stem' has a special meaning, and there is a host of terms used to describe the spore-bearing organs.

However, at this stage the terms that are used to describe the overall structure, rather than those involved in the life-cycle of a fern, are what concern us. They are not difficult, and it is essential that we understand and use them; I must not, and you should not, refer to the 'leaf' of a fern, and we should each try to be as accurate as we can for one another's sake.

Working from below ground upwards, there are several different kinds of rootstocks. The one most of us are familiar with has a sort of tumpy, scaly lump or group of lumps, which is what is left above ground when many different kinds of ferns die down for winter. This is called a *caudex. Dryopteris filix-mas* is an example of a fern with a caudex.

Then there are rhizomes, a term familiar to everyone who grows bearded irises or Solomon's seal. These are roots which proliferate beneath the surface of the soil and give rise to above-ground growths that form no crown. The American oak fern, *Onoclea sensibilis*, grows in this way. The shuttlecock fern, *Matteuccia struthiopteris*, has underground rhizomes that enable it to colonise an area and it also has *caudices* (the plural of *caudex*). I think it may be the only fern that does, but I am not sure.

Most fern rhizomes run fairly close to the surface, but those of bracken are very deep. They are also thick and constitute a formidable food reserve for the plant, which is why you have to be extremely persistent and frequent in getting rid of its top growth. As soon as it has a chance to throw up some more, the roots are fed and lie waiting like some well-nourished monster of the deep.

The leaf of a flowering plant is an organ dedicated to the nourishment of the plant. It contains chlorophyll, the green agent which permits the conversion of carbon dioxide into sugars. Chlorophyll is chillingly close in its chemistry to haemoglobin, a fact that makes me, if nobody else, feel the futility of vanity in human beings. Without these two pigments and one or two odd blue ones there would be no gas exchange in higher creatures and plants, and thus little but the most primitive, mainly uni-cellular life. Ferns contain chlorophyll and are, in terms of the history of the planet, well advanced. That they antedate all flowering plants is a fact upon which it is salutary to dwell.

However, their life-giving green pigment is borne in structures that are not purely dedicated to their nourishment, and cannot therefore be called leaves. On the backs of each green organ will be found others, which contain the reproductive spores, so the whole must be given another name, and this is the *frond*.

If only life could be that simple! Some ferns, such as some osmundas, have separate fronds for the spores, while the rest are spore-free. Thus you have *fertile* and *sterile* fronds. The two kinds usually look quite different; the fertile ones, being concerned not with nutrition, but with reproduction, are narrower and soon become brown with the concentration of spore-bearing organs. Just to be awkward, other osmundas have dual-purpose fronds — upper parts fertile, lower parts sterile.

A frond is divided into two main parts. The lower part only is called the stem, which arises from the rootstock and ends where the green part of the frond begins. Beyond that is the *blade*. The blade has a midrib, which you and I would look upon as an extension of the stem. However, it is called the *rachis*.

The really interesting bit is the blade: this is what we usually, but not always, recognise as ferny. Sometimes it is strap-shaped and undivided, as in the hart's

Top: A splendid colony of the shuttlecock fern, *Matteuccia struthiopteris*. University of Leiden Botanic Garden, Holland. *John Kelly*

Bottom: *Davallia mariesii*, showing how its rootstock gave rise to the name 'hare's foot fern'. Clodagh, Sherkin Island, Co. Cork, Ireland. *John Kelly*

tongue and bird's nest ferns, and these are good starting points from which to embark on the subject of the descriptions of the blades of ferns.

In these two, the term 'strap-shaped' obviously applies to the whole frond. What is important to realise is that ferns are described initially in terms of the overall outline shape of the frond *no matter how deeply and frequently cut or divided it may be.*

Blades may be properly described using the terms that apply to the leaves of flowering plants. They can be linear (rarely), lanceolate, which means shaped like the head of a lance (e.g. *Athyrium filix-femina*), ovate – that is, oval but broadest at a point nearer the base than the centre (*Dryopteris affinis*), oblong, an expression meaning parallel-sided (*Asplenium scolopendrium*), triangular (*Dryopteris dilatata*), elliptic (*Thelypteris limbosperma*) and even trifoliate (*Dryopteris sieboldii*).

Simple blades are described simply. All that is needed is to use one of the above terms or perhaps to combine two, as in linear-oblong, which describes fully the frond of a hart's tongue, which is parallel-sided for much of its length but then becomes much narrower.

Descriptions of compound blades are great fun if you are a fern freak, a necessity if you are the reader of this book and, believe me, a monumental headache if you are its writer. Never mind. If you are to choose the most interesting and appropriate ferns for the various sites in your garden we must get on with it.

What I must first impress upon you is that the coining and use of terms to describe different kinds of fern fronds is not in the interests of obscurity, but of brevity. Each of the 'technical terms' we shall come to has the virtue of compressing into a single word what otherwise would take a whole compound sentence of description.

The simplest kind of compound leaf is the sort in which the blade is repeatedly and regularly cut almost to the rachis. In leaves of flowering plants, cutting is a relative thing that extends from mere tooth-like lobing (dentate margins) to conspicuous lobing, as in American oaks and *Gunnera chilensis*. In ferns it is always decisive and seldom less than half-way to the rachis.

If the cutting of the leaf does not reach the rachis, it is termed 'pinnatifid', which means 'cut like a feather'. The blade will have a crudely feather-like appearance but will still look fairly solid. The divisions of the blade are still recognisably all of a piece. Polypodies have pinnatifid blades.

When the cutting reaches right to the rachis, the frond is termed 'pinnate', which means 'feather-like'. The lover of logic had better give up right here and join the game, as the difference between something that is 'cut like a feather' and something that is just 'like a feather' begins to sound like one of those conundrums which occupy philosophers and contemplators of navels. It is, nevertheless, highly important if you want to discuss ferns, and the botanical terms are best accepted *nem. con.*

The divisions into which a pinnate frond is cut are termed *pinnae*. A pinna may be sessile, in which case its base adheres to the rachis, as in *Blechnum spicant*, or it may have a stalk, as in *Cystopteris fragilis*.

In a pinnate frond the pinnae are entire; that is to say they are undivided. The next stage is when they are divided but not down to their midribs. Once again we have pinnatifid division. In *Dryopteris filix-mas* the fronds are pinnate and the pinnae pinnatifid. This state is termed bipinnatifid, but the word is not often used and it is less muddling to talk about a fern being 'pinnate, pinnae pinnatifid'.

As by now you have, I expect, latched on to this system, you will either have thrown up your hands and gone home or be anxious to see if you are right in predicting what comes next. It is, of course, when the pinnae themselves are pinnate and, lo and behold, the blade is described as *bipinnate*. Simple!

Yes, very well, but we have, I am afraid, hardly started. Firstly, there is a word for this new subdivision, the part of a pinna; it is called a *pinnule*. At this stage, let us take just one species of fern and see what happens.

Polystichum setiferum is the soft shield fern, a very hardy, semi-evergreen, easily grown fern. It is bipinnate, and each pinnule is shaped like a hand in a mitten, with the thumb stuck out. It is very regular and is quite unlike the pinnule of the hard shield fern, *Polystichum aculeatum*, which, although showing something of the same persuasion, looks more like the overall profile of a fat chorus girl trying a high kick.

Suppose now that these pinnules themselves become divided to their midribs. The pinna is now bipinnate! Furthermore, the whole blade is tripinnate. If you think for a moment that this is all academic hogwash or that I am having fun with you in extremely bad taste, just look at the tripinnate forms of our soft shield fern. They are most beautiful and have the quality of Nottingham lace, and are referred to as *divisilobum* in the old system of naming.

This system is now outlawed by international convention, as cultivar names must be in a vernacular language. In other words, a plant which is selected and grown on by vegetative propagation must be given a fancy name in German, English, Tagalog, or whatever, *but not Latin*. This is specifically aimed at such monstrosities in the conifer world as *Chamaecyparis pisifera* 'Squarrosa Cyanoviridis' (now reduced to 'Boulevard' and selling by the hundred thousand), and is a good rule on the whole. However, where ferns are concerned

Polystichum setiferum 'Plumosum'. University Botanic Garden, Cambridge. *John Kelly*

the Latin names provided descriptions that immediately let you know where you were. *Polystichum setiferum divisilobum* was, in nomenclature terms, a nonsense, yet you knew to expect a tripinnate form. In *P.s. plumosum* you looked for one that was quadripinnate: stupendously delicate fronds in which the pinnules, not merely the pinnae, were pinnate — the ultimate in ferniness.

Nowadays we get over the problem by dividing genera into groups. No plant may have more than two consecutive names in Latin (e.g. *Polystichum setiferum*). Any third, given as recognition of further classification in the wild, should be preceded by var., f., ssp. etc., but seldom is when it is gardeners, as opposed to botanists, who are writing them, as none of us can ever remember if the darned thing is a natural variety, form or sub-species. To retain the useful words like 'divisilobum' we now give them capital initial letters as in Divisilobum group.

Thus the plants that used to be called *Polystichum setiferum divisilobum* are now *Polystichum setiferum* Divisilobum group unless they are absolutely specifically named forms within the divisilobum *genre*. In that case they take the name of the group, preferably in brackets, followed by the cultivar name in the vernacular language. An example of this is *Polystichum setiferum* (Divisilobum group) 'Herrenhausen'.

Exceptions to this are allowed where genuine cultivar names, as opposed to what are recognisably group names, were given in Latin before the rules changed. For example, *P.s.* 'Pulcherrimum Bevis' used to be written *P.s. pulcherrimum* 'Bevis'. The 'pulcherrimum' has been recognised as a renowned adjunct to the 'Bevis' and so is retained. In *Athyrium filix-femina* you will find group names and cultivars such as 'Vernoniae Cristatum', which are allowed to remain, but which could not be so dubbed under the present rules.

The pitfalls for those such as this author are many, varied, and efficient. Fern fans everywhere will pick up my mistakes and muddles, and they are welcome to. I believe that the time must come when our ferns should be named more for the gardener than for the fern collector and that the present system is a good one so long as the discipline of inserting the group name is not lost. It is obviously a mess and this is a plea on behalf of myself and my fellow gardeners who enjoy ferns as garden plants that some further thought be given to the problem. Gardening should be a joy, not a garnering to oneself of pseudo-academic status.

Meanwhile, *revenir à nos moutons*, we are by no means through yet. All we have done is to describe the progressive subdivision of fern fronds which, up to the tripinnate stage, occurs freely in nature. *Dryopteris dilatata*, for instance, a reasonably common native of the British Isles, is tripinnate. The next step is to look at mutations in the shapes of the fronds.

Chapter 1 gave a taste of the way in which fern names have been and are conceived. It also noted the way in which British ferns in particular mutate, and a hypothesis to explain it was, if not erected, then hinted at. To have gone farther into these matters at that stage would have meant that nobody would have read this far. That you are interested enough still to be with me means that you are trapped on the train until it emerges from the tunnel.

There are all sorts of variations on the normal states of fern fronds. From time to time mutated forms have proliferated in cultivation, but at the present time we seem to have evolved, in our neo-Lamarckian way, a more empathetic view of the world, such that freaks and oddities do not interest us for the sake of their freakishness or departure from the normal, but mutations are prized if they are beautiful.

There are mutations of the entire shape of the frond which, you will remember, is irrespective of its degree of division or subdivision. There are also variations in the shapes of the pinnules. The third kind has to do with the overall size of the plant.

Athyrium filix-femina 'Frizelliae Cristatum'. *Polystichum setiferum* 'Cristato-pinnulum' is in the background. King's Gatchell, Ottery St Mary, Devon. *John Kelly*

Perversely taking the third first, a change in overall size is, perhaps, the most appealing of all. It is certainly most germane to the selection of ferns for the rock garden and wall. The most perfect example is a form of the lady fern, *Athyrium filix-femina* 'Minutissimum', which is truly and beautifully a miniature. Even when grown in shade and plenty of moisture it is never more than about six inches high, as opposed to the two to three feet of the pure species. It is ideal for the peat wall, so long as it is segregated from incoming sporelings, and it is utterly delightful with erodiums, as it will unfurl its fronds in the middle of their flowering and accompany their charming foliage with its own exquisite grace. It has all the cameo loveliness of a tiny Thai princess.

Unfortunately, changes in size rarely occur on their own. Usually a reduction in size goes with other kinds of change, of which the *congested* is the most usual. In this, the spaces between the pinnae are shortened, so that the whole length of the blade is considerably reduced. The effect is often very attractive, as the pinnae are made to overlap. If you find 'Congestum group' or *congestum* still appearing in a name, you can straight away begin to investigate its fitness for the rock or wall garden. The word 'congested', with its overtones of bronchial troubles, is an unfortunate one; 'foreshortened' would always have been a non-starter, but it describes the phenomenon rather better.

The most common change in frond shape involves cresting. This happens when the tip of a whole frond, or the tips of pinnae or pinnules or combinations of frond tips with other parts, are divided into 'tassels' or formed into thickened, more or less wavy crests.

My favourite crested fern is *Dryopteris affinis* (Cristata group) 'The King', often written as *D.a.* 'Cristata The King'. This shows no reduction in size, but the frond tip has a neat crest and each pinna is crested in just the same way as the tip. This makes for a fine, symmetrical frond that is not a bit freakish. One that appears as *D.a.* 'Congesta Cristata' is a good dwarf for the rock garden, with fronds that are both foreshortened and crested. It is less than a foot high and sometimes half that, depending on conditions.

Asplenium scolopendrium has entire, strap-shaped fronds, and they show a kind of variation that is almost an extension of cresting all round the frond margins. This is denoted in the old-style names by the word *crispum*. There are all sorts of frond changes in this species: sometimes the frond itself branches low down (ramose), and this may be accompanied by cresting, or the surface of the frond may be covered with raised wrinkles (muricate). Occasionally, the frond base, always tending to an auriculate shape, has the auricles expanded so that the frond looks like a large arrow head. This is termed saggitate. When you start looking at varieties of the hart's tongue you will find yourself up against several combinations of these in the names, such as 'Ramo-Cristata' and 'Saggitato-Cristata'.

Persevere, though, as many of them are very beautiful and are among the easiest and toughest of the ferns that you can choose for your wall. They are good in rock gardens, too, but not planted on the flat. They look right in vertical crevices, preferably in some shade.

The best advice that can be given to gardeners who want to make a choice for the rock and wall gardens is to look at the list of species at the end of this chapter and choose any varieties of them that are on the one hand suitable, and on the other hand available at the time. The names should now give you a clue to what to expect if you order by post; catalogue descriptions may be sketchy and you can often fill in the details yourself from the names.

What is certain is that you are highly unlikely to find the right kinds of smaller ferns in garden centres. There is only a small demand for them at the moment, and it is among the handful of excellent specialist nurseries that you are likely to find them. The same does not entirely apply to the ferns for border situations, but it soon will as you become more widely interested in ferns as a whole.

Species and Varieties of Ferns for Rock and Wall Gardens

Adiantum pedatum
Adiantum venustum
Asplenium adiantum-nigrum
Asplenium ruta-muraria
Asplenium scolopendrium
  A.s. 'Marginatum Irregulare' (15–30cm)
  A.s. 'Muricatum' (30cm)
  A.s. 'Ramo-Cristatum' (15cm)
Asplenium trichomanes
  A.t. 'Cristatum' (10cm)
Asplenium viride
Athyrium filix-femina
  A.f-f. 'Frizelliae'(40cm)
  A.f-f. (Cristatum group) 'Gemmatum' (20cm. Red stemmed)
  A.f-f. 'Minutissimum' (10–15cm)
  A.f-f. 'Vernoniae cristatum' (40cm)
Blechnum penna-marina
Blechnum spicant
Ceterach officinarum
Cryptogramma crispa
Cystopteris fragilis
Cystopteris regia
Dryopteris dilatata 'Crispum Whiteside' (30cm)
Dryopteris filix-mas
  D.f-m. 'Crispa' (30–40cm)
  D.f-m. 'Crispa Cristata' (30–40cm)
Dryopteris affinis 'Congesta' (15–20cm)
  D.a. 'Congesta Cristata' (15–20cm)
Gymnocarpium dryopteris
Phegopteris connectilis
Polypodium vulgare and *P. australe*
  P.v. 'Bifidum Cristatum' (20cm)
  P.v. 'Interjectum' (30cm)
Polystichum setiferum
  P.s. 'Congestum' (15–20cm)
  P.s. 'Plumoso-Divisilobum' (25–30cm)
Thelypteris phegopteris

Dryopteris affinis 'Congesta' in a shady, leafy corner. Kells House, Co. Kerry, Ireland.
John Kelly

7

Ferns in the Mixed Border

THERE IS, I think, a distinctive gardening style that has developed during the late twentieth century. It arises from the interest gardeners have in plants, as opposed to mere flowers.

In the days of Victoria Sackville-West, Gertrude Jekyll, William Robinson, and others who may be said either to have belonged to, been deeply influenced by, or have themselves influenced the Arts and Crafts Movement, colour schemes were paramount. Structure was largely given by garden features – hedges, walls, buildings, and so on – which was why Jekyll and Lutyens worked so well together. To this day, the Jekyll-esque garden and the Lutyens house at Les Moutiers, in Varengeville, France, complement one another perfectly and the house seems to need the hedges and pergolas that divide the garden space.

The garden of today, however, can stand alone. That is not to say that all gardens of this era are similar; far from it. There is room for all styles and kinds of gardens, but each age has its own style and its own vanguard. In ours the recognition of the plant as a whole and not just as a bearer of flowers is the keynote in a liberation of the garden from its previous divisions into departments – herbaceous border, shrubbery, even fernery.

Now that we do not rely on painting with flowers but rather build up character in our gardens by allowing the plants themselves to impose a structure and order in which the subtleties of form, stem and trunk colour, leaf shapes and foliage tints, and the excitement of flowering as an event, rather than just a filling in of a numbered square, can all play their parts, demarcation has gone out of the window. It does not matter that *Rosa rubrifolia* is a shrub or that *Dierama pulcherrimum* is a subshrub that behaves like an herbaceous perennial; what we care about is that the two plants, particularly when a purple-flowered

Polystichum setiferum 'Pulcherrimum Druery' in the background with *Pittosporum tenuifolium* 'Garnettii' and the deep green *Hebe azurens*. *Dryopteris filix-mas* 'Jackson' is in the foreground. King's Gatchell, Ottery St Mary, Devon. *John Kelly*

form of the dierama is used, strike sparks off one another like Gertrude Lawrence and Noel Coward.

The mixed border has arrived or, if it had arrived before, it has been recognised and codified. It is a more subtle way of gardening than the herbaceous border and one with infinitely more interest in the colder months. It is also greatly more cheerful than the shrubbery, or shrub border, which was so often deadly in summer. And it is more difficult, but infinitely more satisfying to carry out than either.

The mixed border has allowed the use of ferns in the main part of the garden, if one can put it that way. There was no place for ferns in the herbaceous border, where colour was everything. Even if there had been, what a sorry sight they would have been in winter, with the persistent ones beaten down by wind and snow and, pathetically naked on the bare soil, exposed to every icy blast! Millions of years of evolution would have screamed from every cell of any plant subject to such abuse. In the shrubbery, the odd fern might have been allowed a dowdy, neglected existence on the grounds that it was better than permitting weeds to colonise the soil. Occasionally one saw old specimens among even older shrubs, the legacy of some gardener who had learned his craft between the wars and had moved on, his property passing to those with time only to keep the lawns trimmed and the car washed.

In the mixed border there is shelter from wind throughout the year. Ferns are not made to look forlorn and old-maidish among the bright young things of the flower catalogue, but instead bring a lush freshness to their neighbours, hiding the indignity of spindly stems, disguising the embarrassment of sparse foliage, and drawing a decent veil over quarrelling neighbours.

The other plants, because they can be relied upon to stand firm and not cravenly to flop just when needed most, provide the shade that the ferns need and prevent the soil from becoming dry. We have learned to use the mutual support of plants, so that visitors to a large public garden in the south of England can see *Cotinus coggygria* 'Foliis Purpureis' spreading finger-like branches along the soil, between which *Lilium regale*, roots cool and heads in sun, appears as grateful as the *Dryopteris* species that take mid-day shade from its raised centre.

Fascinating plant associations have been made possible, using the ambience of the mixed border, but the baby should not be lost with the bath water, and those that depend on shade must not be forgotten. If they can be incorporated in the mixed border, so much the better.

'Border' is probably a misnomer, covering 'beds' and all sorts of other plots as well. The late twentieth-century gardener is losing contact with the exactness of such terms and it does not concern him. A bed or a border, a plot or 'the bit behind the greenhouse' are just map references. What he is interested in is the interplay of plants.

If the shady companions of ferns are remembered, some of their ravishing associations can soon become dearly loved and important elements in the under storey of the mixed border. Trilliums and lady ferns (*Athyrium filix-femina*) make as classic a pairing as graces any peat wall garden, and yet are as perfectly suited to the mixed border as they are to the woodland floor. A lightly crested, and perhaps not too invasive form of *Dennstaedtia punctilobula*, making a lacy, tousled colony, is a perfect foil for the gorgeous, deep sky-blue of *Meconopsis grandis*, but this need not be confined to a peat or woodland garden. It works just as well in the well-judged spaces between lightly-limbed shrubs, where shafts of sunlight can add chiaroscuro to the scene and, in the evening, lend an uncanny dazzle to the blue.

The coming of the mixed border has been gradual. So gradual indeed that people find it hard to think of it as anything special. Surely it has always been around! In fact, it is so new (new, that is, in the relative world of gardening in

Ferns, primulas and arum lilies. Bramble Cottage, Ottery St Mary, Devon. *John Kelly*

which labels, unchanged, become wrong for a while and then once more correct) that writers on ferns still tend to restrict themselves to advocating nothing but peaty, woodsy partnerships for ferns.

The mixed border is not the same thing as the mixed fern border, in which ferns are the main theme and dominate, while their associates are secondary, although complementary. The mixed fern border was a great advance on the fernery and a major step in the recognition of ferns as garden plants, but it had the same drawback as the purpose-made fern rock garden; integration of ferns into the garden as a whole was not envisaged.

In sociological terms the difference is a little like enclaves of immigrants in a country. Whether they are Russian Jews in New York, Irish in Boston or Ealing, or any of the present-day communities in, say, Miami or Bradford, the tendency is for them to accrete in one or two areas, in which they can create their own specialised environment. Integration only really takes place when they are evenly scattered among the 'indigenous' population, whose lives are thereby enriched and made more colourful.

The mixed border represents the true assimilation of ferns into the garden

Cystopteris fragilis, the brittle bladder fern. University Botanic Garden, Cambridge. *John Kelly*

population, to the benefit of both. The gardener's attitude to them changes, too, so that ferns belong in the wider category of 'plants' and thus receive their proper due. Some nurseries, whose stock has previously excluded ferns, already make a feature of them in catalogues that are household names.

In Holland, where they understand things about plants that other nations often neglect, ferns already play parts in the average suburban garden that most of us have never as much as thought of. Shuttlecock, lady and male ferns can be seen in gardens that have no pretensions whatever to be anything other than ordinary. They grow among petunias, lobelias, clarkias, and mesembryanthemums with an aplomb that would amaze not only the Victorians, but most gardeners of modern times. Shuttlecock ferns are used as exclamation marks in full sun (but always with plenty of moisture), lady ferns bedeck sunny rockeries, and polypodies wave their short, handsome fronds from every nook and cranny.

This is not high horticulture, nor is it always the first thrust of good garden design. It is an indication that we have missed the boat with ferns because we have failed to understand them. To grow finely divided forms of soft shield fern among zonal pelargoniums may not be everyone's ideal — indeed, they are far

Aspleniums and erodiums. King's Gatchell, Ottery St Mary, Devon. *John Kelly*

more appropriately planted alongside *Helleborus orientalis* – but it does show a liberation of the mind from the strict demarcation that we still fall heir to. As a matter of fact, such a combination is not so far from that which is praised in hanging baskets, when an asparagus fern may be used. You may think bright flowers and ferny foliage in a hanging basket is a bit trite, but other people do not.

The search for 'ground cover' plants is one of the less attractive aspects of modern gardening. The well-known saying, 'Cover your ground or Nature will cover it for you', is true enough, but it is surely preferable to make as close a study of the ground level of the garden as you would any other, rather than to put in rampant ivies and periwinkles that are not only boring but soon become a nuisance.

One sees all too often a fern, possibly a hangover from a previous owner of the garden, struggling as ivy swarms over its caudex and sends lethal tentacles obscenely exploring its dainty fronds. That the fern, divided to make a small community, would cover the ground in a far more elegant manner and constitute a far more plantsmanlike planting, is seldom thought of.

There is little that is more entrancing as 'ground cover' than the year-round glossiness of *Asplenium scolopendrium*. It is the perfect foil for all kinds of flowers and complements the foliage of most shrubs. Whether it is the wide, equally glossy, palm-like leaves of *Fatsia japonica* (a shrub that is hardy out of the wind, even though it looks positively tropical), or the deep maroon-mahogany of *Cotinus* 'Velvet Cloak', association with this hardy, winter-persistent fern is a bonus indeed.

Plants at ground level in the mixed border should not be obvious in their station in life. The border should have depth in the vertical sense as well as height and width. Interest should not stop somewhere below the level of the flowers of the perennials, or only arise when spring bulbs draw attention away from the general bareness. The interplay of persistent ferns and those that unfurl their fronds in spring is a factor that can lend fascination to the lower levels and stimulate the planting of other choice, but lowly plants.

The glossiness of the hart's tongue makes it the ideal foil for the filigree fronds of less 'butch' ferns. It also contrasts tellingly with other entire, undivided shapes, such as the leaves of hostas, as their matt, waxy surfaces and tendencies towards blue and grey tones are completely different. The bright shininess of the hart's tongue fern surrounding a good specimen of *Hosta sieboldiana* 'Elegans' does a great deal to accentuate its big leaves that are so much like elephant hide. A combination of flowering plant and ferny leaves is found in *Anemonopsis macrophylla*, whose flowers are like spurless aquilegias in mauvy purple, and this is perfectly at home at close quarters with the hart's tongue, especially in a rich, moist soil in the shade of a shrub — a situation that is part and parcel of a mixed border.

It would be a mistake to relegate ferns to an entirely subsidiary role in the mixed border, however. Such a feature is best made to have an undulating profile, so that the shrubs and trees it contains do not dominate its outline throughout, but are absent here and there or restricted to those of lesser heights.

In these glades, the occasional tall fern, its roots cooled by surrounding flowering plants of lower stature, can be allowed to flaunt itself as an accent plant, making a bold, statement about ferniness and ferndom. *Dryopteris affinis* is an excellent one to choose, whose fronds can be four feet long when the plant is well fed and provided with the dappled shade of the nearby shrubs. Its regular pinnae, fresh greenness and bold stance strike a completely different note from the other denizens of the border and also act as a visual clue, drawing attention to other ferns.

I confess to having completely overlooked the fern content of a border in a French garden. The planting was subtle, but the eye was drawn to the exquisite combinations of flower colours and the delightful use of shape and form. Once a fern or two were pointed out, it became apparent that there were many and some of them were most interesting. On reflection, a strong fern 'marker', perhaps even at an end of the border or planted in a bay, might have resulted in the observer's being able the better to appreciate the nuances of what was, in all other respects, a masterly piece of gardening.

One of the mistakes that is made in incorporating ferns into mixed borders is to neglect to allow them enough room. Ferns depend for their allure to a large extent upon their gracefully curved fronds, and an untidy fern looks weedy very quickly. As soon as a fern runs out of space, its fronds become hitched and snagged on nearby branches and the midribs crack, so that fronds look distorted and as distressing as birds do when their wings are broken.

Furthermore, single ferns never have the majesty of a group. If you plant one that can be divided, it is no bad thing to allow room for two or three to develop, as each single crown resulting from division will have a grace that older, multi-crowned plants often lack. The space can be taken up by perennials for a few years or even annuals. Those of us who may be the greatest snobs about annuals could not deny the elegance of, say, *Nicotiana* 'Lime Green', as aristocratic a filler-in of spaces as you could possibly wish for.

The pure fern border is not a garden feature that I would decry in any way. If it is well made and assiduously looked after, it can be a delightful surprise and a deliciously cool, restful one at that. It is not likely to be very large, as the necessary conditions of shade, moisture and a good, deep, leafy soil are unlikely to extend for very far. If they do, you have, not a fern border, but a woodland garden — a different thing altogether.

However, it is my experience that gardeners who plant fern borders – not all of them, but most – cannot resist putting the odd trillium, meconopsis, or galanthus with them. The desire to create plant associations is irresistible in most of us, and gradually the border becomes a mixed fern border. If it is a small one, it will not advance beyond this stage, as the scope for the larger, woody plants is not there. However, if it is larger, and the glossy, deep green, trifoliate leaves of *Choisya ternata* seem inevitably to be drawn to the side of the lady fern, and the wine-tinted, simple greenery of *Vaccinium glauco-album* demands to be set down to live alongside the neatness of *Polystichum setiferum* 'Acutilobum', what gardener worth his or her salt can deny them?

8

Fern Reproduction in Nature and the Garden

WHEN I was a sixth-form schoolboy – and we were, I regret to say, all boys – I took botany and was very good at it. I was also terrible at physics and still find equations and things frightening, so I am not bragging of my prowess at the study of plants, merely hinting that one's lifetime loves may, with any luck, match what talents one has.

The master in charge of botany was a sweet-natured but firm man called Gaman. He was a fine teacher, too. As a junior I never knew why he was called 'Chaps' Gaman; he certainly neither rode Western style nor suffered, as far as I know, from chilblains. It was only later that I learned that he would introduce the main headlines of botany with preliminary announcements such as, 'Hi, chaps! Photosynthesis!'

In all my lessons with him save one, he never did this, and I began to think his legend apocryphal until the magical day dawned in the month of the Coronation of Her Majesty Queen Elizabeth II. At that momentous time, when Sir Edmund Hillary conquered Everest and Sir Gordon Richards rode his longed-for and universally popular first Derby winner, Mr Gaman announced at the beginning of his lesson, 'Hi, chaps! Alternation of generations!'

That I still recall it is remarkable. What is far more noteworthy is that I remember the contents of that lesson and the ones that followed as if they were yesterday. Perhaps it was 'Chaps' Gaman who fired the spark in the tinder of my childhood fascination with wallflowers and antirrhinums on rockwork; he is certainly responsible for my interest in ferns. I hope he is still alive; he would be eighty-four as I write.

Alternation of generations describes the astonishing method of reproduction of ferns in nature. There are two separate kinds of fern plants, each totally different, for each species. One is what we recognise as a fern, with its caudex or rhizome, stem, rachis and blade; the other is a tiny, primitive scale of green tissue, much like a liverwort, with nothing remotely recognisable as a fern at all.

Unless you understand it, you have little hope of raising ferns from spores or of avoiding disturbing all but the tiny minority of reproducing ferns in your garden. However, it is not difficult, and I am as fascinated by it as I was in that far-off year; the year in which I had my first glass of champagne.

There is a chicken-and-egg conundrum involved; which came first, the fern as we know it, or the green scale? I have no idea and such a question is yet another that the philosophers can go away and earn their salaries on. What we can do is to break in somewhere, and the best place is with the mature fern plant, fronds and all.

Let us take a *Dryopteris* species, something like the common British male fern. Anything more specific would tax too far my ability to recall Mr Gaman's superb blackboard drawings, which I reproduced to great effect in my examinations. Its fronds are pinnate, and the pinnae pinnatifid.

If you look at the backs of mature fern fronds, you will see varying arrangements of brown bits, according to species. In some, such as *Asplenium scolopendrium*, they are long, thin and arranged herringbone fashion like tribal scars. In others, such as the male ferns, they are small, round, and arranged usually in two rows on each pinnule.

These are groups of spore-bearing organs and are called *sori*, of which the singular is *sorus*. What you actually see may not be the sorus itself, but a membrane wholly or partly covering it. This is called the *indusium*. Each sorus may contain fifty or so *sporangia*, each of which is an independent organ containing sixty-four spores (one, doubled five times).

If each sorus has fifty sporangia, each sporangium sixty-four spores, each pinnule ten sori, each pinna eighteen spore-bearing pinnules, each blade twenty-eight spore-bearing pinnae, and each plant ten spore-bearing fronds, then the plant will produce one hundred and sixty-one and a quarter million spores. That we are not neck deep in ferns world-wide is a measure of how many fail to find good germination sites.

Each sporangium is like a ball on a stalk. It is highly susceptible to drying out, which is why the indusium is there, to keep it from doing so. Once the sporangia are ripe, the indusia begin to peel away, and that is why you usually see incomplete indusia on mature fern fronds.

As the cells of the wall of the sporangium are exposed to the drying influence of the air, some of them, which form a crest on its surface and have thickened walls that are highly sensitive to moisture changes, become energised. When

Dryopteris affinis, showing sori. Abbotsbury Gardens, Dorset. *John Kelly*

their water content drops to a certain level they reverse their curvature and the whole sporangium pings open as if on a spring hinge, releasing the spores into the air.

The sori and indusia are diagnostic elements in determining the species of ferns. This is of little interest to us except in as much as it explains why names like 'soft shield' are used. They refer to the shapes of the sori, which are severally shield-, buckler-, bladder-shaped, and so on.

The fern plant as we know it is called the *sporophyte*, which means the plant that bears the spores. Each of its cells contains the diploid number of chromosomes, which is denoted by the symbol 2n. In *Dryopteris filix-mas*, 2n = 164; In *Polystichum setiferum*, 2n = 82. Each spore, on the other hand, contains the haploid number of chromosomes, which is half the diploid number; n = 82 for the former species and n = 41 for the second.

The split between generations occurs at the point of formation of the spore, when reduction division leads to the halving of the chromosome number. In higher plants, reduction division occurs at the formation of pollen and ova, which are then separately dispersed and are free to encounter their opposite

Sori on *Dryopteris erythrosora*. King's Gatchell, Ottery St Mary, Devon. *John Kelly*

numbers from other individuals, after which they unite to form a seed. Not so in ferns.

The spore, alighting on a suitable piece of ground, germinates. Germination is not the right word, as the *germ-* part refers to seeds, and ferns have no seeds, but it is convenient to use it. What happens is that the spore undergoes successive cell division, eventually forming a green, heart-shaped scale, only three or four cells thick and about one eighth of an inch (3mm) across. This scale is called the *prothallus*, and is the *gametophyte* generation of the plant; all its cells have the haploid number of chromosomes. On its lower surface there develop sex organs of two types. The female organs, called *archegonia*, produce egg cells, while the male ones, the *antheridia*, manufacture motile male cells with cilia (mobile whiskers) with which they swim in the film of water on the surface of the prothallus. The male and female cells are called *gametes*; hence gametophyte.

Incest now takes place, or perhaps one could call it hermaphroditism. Whatever it may be, it is far enough for a tiny, single cell to swim from one end of the prothallus to another without having to reach another prothallus in order

to do its job. To do so would be, for a male gamete, something akin to a man's determining to swim from Fishguard to Rosslare, or across Lake Erie; not entirely impossible, but virtually so. What this means is that hybridisation between species is extremely rare in cultivation and much more so in the wild, where no ferry is at hand.

Secretions of malic acid urge the gamete on to efforts of its cilia reminiscent of a quinquireme of Ancient Greece, until its mission ends at the source, which is an archegonium. Darwinism's dicta may indeed be fulfilled when the strongest swimmers, finding the seas unusually calm and the currents favourable, make the trip from their ripe antheridia and, finding their own archegonia unready, launch themselves upon the friendly dew and land upon a nearby prothallus from another individual, which is almost always of the same species.

Union having been achieved, the fertilised egg, whose cells now contain both sets of chromosomes and are now diploid, begin to divide to form an embryo sporophyte. The embryo grows to make a tiny fern plant with primitive fronds that look rather like miniature ginkgo leaves and then finally, recognisably characteristic fronds, although still minute, appear. It is at this stage that we crass humans recognise it as a fern again, having been in ignorance of this wonderful process for all but the last century or so of our existence. The alternation of generations is complete.

Propagation of Ferns

There are several aspects of this strange and wonderful method of reproduction that are highly significant for the propagation of ferns by spores. One is that there is a great deal of material. Another is that, because the spores derive directly from the tissues of the sporophyte, they *must* be true to type. Therefore, so long as they are not contaminated at a later stage by the presence of spores from other species, they *must* breed 'true' unless they are mutant varieties.

Consequently, great care has to be taken to ensure that such contamination does not occur. Not only that; an invasion of spores from, say, bracken, which 'germinate' with great avidity, leads to the overwhelming of any desirable prothalli and complete failure. If you think that wild fern spores are not going to arrive, just try putting a pot of pure, moist sphagnum peat outside in the shade for a year. If it fails to end up with a fern growing in it, it will be an unusual event.

Other plant life can invade as well. Mosses are hard to repel from a medium that is congenial to the functioning of a prothallus. Worst of all are liverworts. To a prothallus, a liverwort scale is about the same as the 'Close Encounters'

Fronds of *Phymatosorus scolopendria* with sori. Kells House, Co. Kerry, Ireland.
Nicola Kelly

flying saucer would be to us. Obviously, such events must be prevented. The question is, how?

Above all, a sterile procedure needs to be set up. Firstly, wash your hands thoroughly. Secondly, use brand new plastic pots or clay ones that have been thoroughly scrubbed. Thirdly, sterilise the soil.

The best soil is, I am quite convinced, a peat-based compost — a proprietary one will do, but it must be at the strength for seed raising. Others whose results I cannot but admire advocate mixtures of sand, leafmould and 'loam'. I am never sure about loam, but good garden soil, never clay, at about one third of the mixture, with one fifth being sharp sand and the rest leafmould, seems to be a consensus recipe. My own results are far better with a soil-less compost than a soil-based one.

It is a mistake for the amateur to use pots that are too small. I am not being snobbish in using the term: an amateur usually has calls on his or her time that lead to the possibility of dryness occurring, which is fatal, and the larger soil mass will be less likely to become dry. However, you will not want the pots to be too large, either, as they will simply take up too much room and deplete your compost stores far too quickly.

The best kind of pot is a plastic half-pot about four inches (10 cm) in diameter, but it must be of the sort that will withstand being doused in boiling water. If you cannot obtain such pots, which is unlikely, you will have to use clay ones instead. Acquire some blotting paper, or if that is totally unobtainable, some coffee filter paper. Describe a four-inch circle on it with a child's compass, and cut to the line. It is quite a good idea to mass-produce them once and for all and store them somewhere dry, as it is a tedious job.

Fill a pot to within half an inch of the top with the compost. As with planting ferns in pots, there is no need to put crocks or other drainage material in the bottom: if your compost is well made it will be well drained. Remember, though, that clay pots, with their large drainage holes, need to have a piece of broken pot placed over each hole, concave side downwards, in order to prevent the compost being washed out of the pot.

The compost should — in the case of ferns only, for it is otherwise a fussy practice — be firmed down gently, not with your fingers but with something smooth and round. The bottom of another pot is as good as anything. With clean hands, place a filter disc on the surface of the compost and then slowly pour boiling water over it. Keep doing this until the whole thing is too hot to handle, and then put a clean piece of glass over it. Condensation will immediately occur, but this is nothing to worry about.

When the pot has cooled thoroughly, remove the glass, wipe it dry with a clean cloth or kitchen paper and, *with recently washed hands*, removed the filter paper. Replace the glass immediately.

Allow the moisture content in the pot to settle down, which only takes a few hours. Then take the glass off and dry it as before and sow a tiny amount of spores evenly over the surface of the compost. You can use your clean fingers or a sterilised spatula or the tip of a table knife. Shaking the packet and tapping the spores out is not a method that leads to even sowing.

Then replace the glass and label the pot. What I like to do — and I use plastic pots — is to write on the glass and the pot with the sort of pen that is sold at camera shops for labelling transparency mountings. There is not much room between glass and compost for a conventional label. With clay pots, a number in wax crayon can co-ordinate with a list on the potting-shed wall. From now onwards, allow condensation on the glass to remain, as it will circulate from the glass to the compost and back again.

You must be patient. 'Germination' is haphazard and even the best conditions of a cool atmosphere in a shady place may not produce results for some months. The first sign will be a faint green film on the surface of the compost, but even this should not make you relax. Something just may have gone wrong and it could be moss marshalling its forces to wreck everything. However, if you have not done anything silly like peeking and forgetting to put the glass back, the film should resolve itself in a few weeks into prothalli, and a few more weeks after that should see the first minute fronds which, so long as they are not bracken, are extremely exciting.

Bracken spores are very hard to destroy and do sometimes occur in peat. Unfortunately this is hard to avoid, as peat bogs and bracken are usually found near one another. Their possible presence provides a strong argument against my preference for soil-less composts, and I must admit that I have raised too many pots of bracken for comfort and feel bound to mention it while still maintaining that, in general, peat-based composts seem preferable.

When the young plants are large enough to handle, you can prick them out into the sort of seed trays that have transparent plastic domes over them. If you get the ones whose domes have ventilators, the sporelings can gradually be weaned from the close atmosphere they started in, as the ventilators are gradually opened. Finally, the domes can be removed and the ferns potted on individually.

Thick sowing of the spores is the biggest fault of all. All that effort will result in a generous production of prothalli, only for them to be so closely packed that they cannot develop properly and eventually they just wither and die. Reginald Kaye advocates pricking off little groups of prothalli and allowing

A natural fern nursery on a mossy, moist, woodland bank. Kells House, Co. Kerry, Ireland. *John Kelly*

them to grow on and I have tried this without success. My eyesight is not sufficiently good, even though my manual dexterity is fine and my hands do not shake (well, not from Monday to Friday, anyway), so I cannot recommend this procedure from my own experience. However, it works for him, so do try it, but first do your best to sow sparsely, not just thinly. The spores in a minute pinch may number thousands, and you probably only want half a dozen plants in the end.

There are two ways of obtaining spores. One is to send for them from a fern society's exchange scheme or from a reputable commercial seedsman. Fern spores, with a few exceptions, remain viable for many years, and you should receive them in good condition. The exceptions are some of the ferns that have separate, fertile fronds, such as osmundas, and tree ferns. Spores of the former, and particularly the osmundas, remain viable for only a few days, while tree fern spores are more than usually sensitive to dryness and high temperatures.

The other way is to collect your own. Some people examine the fronds to see that the indusia are coming away or have gone. You can see this with a strong hand lens perfectly well, and you can also see the individual sporangia,

Four-year-old sporelings of *Dicksonia antarctica*. Abbotsbury Gardens, Dorset. *John Kelly*

which look like the crowded filaments in a scouring pad. At this stage the spores are ready for collection — or, rather the sporangia are.

I collect mine in a plastic bag. I remove the frond when it is dry and, depending on its size, put it or individual pinnae in the bag, which I then inflate and tie at the neck. After a few days smudges will appear on the surface of the plastic and these are collections of spores. A shake of the bag collects them in its corner, and when I have enough I take the green bits out and store the rest in a stamp-collector's transparent envelope until needed, or sow them right away.

There are other methods. A very good one involves folding the pinnae or other frond parts into clean, new, white paper. This has the advantage of allowing you to see the spores distinctly, as they are almost always black, tan, or reddish brown. You can scrape the sori from the backs of the fronds with a sharp knife if you like and sow the lot. I have seen this method used to great effect but am always afraid that I shall accidentally remove some green material that will eventually rot and set up a fungal infection.

Some of the mutant varieties of ferns come fairly true from spores, so it is worth collecting and sowing them. However, you must be ruthless in throwing out those that do not, except for the one in a thousand or two that just might be superior. Unfortunately, you need quite a lot of experience before you can make such judgements, but it is something to bear in mind. More immediately, however, you should watch out for the sorts of plants from which you are collecting spores. They should themselves be true to type. If they are species, they should be free from uneven, occasional cresting or other mutational trends, otherwise the sporelings will be likely to be a mess of partly deformed fronds along with normal ones. The gardener who needs to read this chapter really needs also to acquire more fern-time before embarking on anything but the simplest propagation by spores. It is, by any standards, interesting enough.

Propagation by division is quite easy and is applicable to a great many species and varieties. Ferns that have caudices and make clumps can look much less dramatic as they age and their fronds spray out in all directions. If they can be reduced to just one crown they will look much better and have something more of the appeal of the shuttlecock fern. They can be treated just as if they were border perennials, to the extent that the old back-to-back forks trick works perfectly well.

Just in case you have never tried this, it is worth mentioning how to do it. With an old, tough clump, whose root mass may be considerably more than a foot wide, you simply ram a garden fork downwards into its heart. Taking another fork, you turn it so that it is back-to-back with the first one and push it in as well, right next to the other one's tines. The handles will now stand out from one another at about thirty degrees. Now apply pressure *inwards* on the two handles. Sometimes this alone will be enough to separate a clump, but not usually with ferns. Pressure on the handles *outwards* follows, and you may have to repeat both movements a couple of times before the plant splits in two. The next split — dividing each half into two more — is much easier and after it you should be able to complete the division of the fern by hand.

This will often entail cutting the rootstock, and you should do this with a sharp, clean knife. No gardening operation is safe with a knife as blunt as a stick. Sharpness equals safety, unless you are as idiotic as I was the day I took an azalea cutting in ultra close-up on television and gave the camera a screenful of bloody thumb. Luckily it was on tape and has only been seen by BBC staff at Christmas parties!

When you have reduced the old plant to a handful of single crowns, each one should be cleaned of any dead material that might set up rotting. Then you can either pot them up or plant them in a gritty, leafy nursery bed in shade for a year, after which you can lift them for planting in their permanent homes.

Methods of propagation involving the use of tissue at the bases of fronds, are, I believe, effective, but I have never tried them. I have, however, had good results using fronds of varieties of *Polystichum setiferum* and adopting a technique that is more often used for house plants.

In the very finely divided forms of this species, and in some tropical and sub-tropical ferns, bulbils are formed at the bases of the pinnae, close to the midribs. If you remove a frond and peg it down in a seed tray on moist leafmould to which a little sand has been added, the bulbils, which are small, green balls with scales on, gradually put forth roots which are followed by new fronds. The frond itself will rot away, leaving the individual youngsters ready for potting on.

Ferns raised from bulbils will, of course, be true to type. If you want to go in for hybridising ferns, looking for something new, then you can, but it is tricky and involves persuading male gametes from the prothalli of one species to meet up with female gametes of another. There are techniques that you can learn, but such sophisticated processes are beyond the scope of this book.

9

Fern File

MOST OF the ferns mentioned in this chapter can be grown in the open garden all year round or for a significant part of the year. In other words, plants whose proper place is in the house or conservatory, such as the varieties of *Adiantum raddianum*, the house plant maidenhair fern, are not described here even though they may have been mentioned in passing elsewhere.

The Fern File does not pretend to the status of a comprehensive list. Ferns that are very difficult to obtain have been omitted, since this is a book for general gardeners and not for collectors. All the plants mentioned should be obtainable, even if something of a search has to be mounted and perhaps a wait for a year or two undertaken while propagation takes place.

The term 'persistent' has been used in place of 'evergreen', as it is more accurate. Ferns that lose their fronds when in the open but keep them under glass, or those that keep them in mild winters but lose them otherwise, are described as 'semi-persistent'. Those that habitually lose their fronds in winter are referred to as 'deciduous'.

ADIANTUM. Maidenhair ferns

A. capillus-veneris

Northern and Southern Hemispheres in tropical, sub-tropical and warm temperature regions. In the British Isles it is a rare fern in the wild and uncommon in cultivation. It has a creeping, black rhizome and fronds of up to a foot long arise from it at quite close intervals. The stems are black and the blades are bipinnate of tripinnate. Each pinnule is fan-shaped, ragged-edged along the outside, and has a distinct, wiry stalk.

It is not a good plant for the open garden, as it is sensitive to frost. However,

Adiantum venustum. Kells House, Co. Kerry, Ireland. *John Kelly*

in a cold greenhouse with occasional heating it should do well in a pot. The taller form *banksianum* is hardier but still susceptible to anything more than a hint of frost. Semi-persistent.

A. pedatum
There are several forms of this North American fern, all of which are excellent, hardy garden plants. Their blade formation is different from the foregoing species, as it is branched on one side only and in a curve radiating from a central point, so that it is reminiscent of a bird's foot (hence *pedatum*). Each branch has ten to fifteen pairs of pinnules, which are not on distinct stalks. The stems are deep purple. Deciduous.

The species is not hard to grow, given a good fern soil and some small stones among which to shelter its rhizome. It will take a good deal of sun as long as the roots are kept cool and moist.

A. p. aleuticum is a congested form with the pinnules crowded on the fronds and overlapping.

A. p. subpumilum minimum is a dwarf form of about six inches, ideal for the rock garden.

A. venustum
Himalaya. This extremely beautiful fern has triangular fronds which are tripinnate and up to a foot long. The pinnules are fan-shaped, minutely toothed on the outer curve. The fronds turn brown in autumn but are not dropped until spring, then the new ones are produced. It is thus only deciduous in the way that common beech is.

It is a perfectly hardy plant, accused unfairly at times of being invasive but in fact a friendly if rapid coloniser of rich fern soils with good stony shelter for the rhizomes, which must be close to the surface of the soil. In these conditions it requires no more light than part shade.

ASPLENIUM. Spleenworts

A. adiantum-nigrum
This fern is native to Asia, Africa, North America, and Europe, including the British Isles, where it is known as the black spleenwort. It is very variable in size, depending on the conditions in which it finds itself, and the frond can be as short as three or four inches and as long as twelve or fourteen. The fronds are leathery, dark green, triangular and bipinnate to tripinnate. The pinnae are the same shape as the blade and the lower ones only are stalked. Persistent.

This fern grows on the same stable wall in my yard in south-western Ireland as *A. trichomanes*, having germinated in minute cracks in what is by no means a ruin. It is a fine plant for the rock garden, especially in vertical crevices. It may not actually need old mortar, but it is a good idea to bow to the best advice and add it to the soil anyway. It will certainly help the drainage, if nothing else. It becomes less easy to grow the farther east you go and seems to need the moister atmosphere of the more maritime west. In East Anglia it is virtually impossible.

A. ceterach (see *Ceterach officinarum*)

A. ruta-muraria. Wall rue
Found in the British Isles, North America and Asia. The fronds have a distinct blue-green cast in some cases; in others they vary from dark to light green. The fronds are bipinnate with spade-shaped pinnules. It is small, the fronds rarely exceeding four inches in length.

Asplenium scolopendrium. University Botanic Garden, Cambridge. *John Kelly*

This is not an easy plant to grow, but succeeds in vertical crevices in the rock garden so long as the soil is stony and limy.

A. scolopendrium. Hart's tongue
To the older generations of gardeners this will be known as *Phyllitis scolopendrium*, and there is a fair threat that it will become so again. However, the authoritative consensus includes it in *Asplenium* for now.

The stems of the fronds are very short in comparison with the blades and arise from the root stock in a close-coupled ring. The cordate (heart-shaped) bases of the fronds are evenly distant along the stems so that the observer looking down on the plant sees at its centre a most attractive, regular pattern, similar to that seen in *A. nidus*, the bird's nest fern, which is so delightful a plant for house and conservatory.

The fronds are also similar in all respects but size, as those of the hart's tongue are much smaller in general but can be as much as three feet long. The blades are leathery, glossy, entire, strap-shaped, bright green and persistent. The sori are conspicuous, long, raised brown ridges in herringbone patterns.

Asplenium scolopendrium 'Cristatum'. King's Gatchell, Ottery St Mary, Devon. *John Kelly*

The hart's tongue is easy to grow and prefers dappled shade. It is in nature a plant of limestone formations but occurs on acid ones as well. In cultivation it is just as good on an acid loam with camellias and azaleas as it is on limestone with viburnums and tree peonies.

A.s. Crispum group includes several forms with frond edges crimped into frills. They have all occurred naturally and carry no sori. Usually under two feet in height.

A.s. Cristatum group are plants with fronds crested at the tips into fans or corymbs (flat-topped or somewhat dome-shaped). Usually under eighteen inches in height.

A.s. Ramo-cristatum group; spore-raised plants with much-branched fronds ending in corymbose crests.

A.s. Undulatum group. The commonest variation in the species. The fronds are wavy to a greater or lesser degree. In a well-established colony, many sporelings will show this tendency.

Other varieties are available from time to time, such as 'Kaye's Lacerated', which comes true from spores and is therefore not hard to find. The fronds are unusually short and broad, less than a foot long and up to one third as wide, the margins are lacerated and the tips slightly crested.

A. trichomanes. The maidenhair spleenwort
A delightfully pretty plant from northern Europe, Asia and America, including the British Isles, where it is common, except in areas of any industrial pollution. The fronds are simply pinnate; each pinna (of which there may be more than thirty pairs) is broadly oval-oblong and only a quarter of an inch long. The stems are black and the pinnae are light green to ochre-green.

The fronds vary from two inches or so in cracks in walls to a foot where they may be furnished with adequate soil, such as on a rock ledge or in the rock garden. It has few equals for a rock-garden crevice, where its fronds will turn to grow upwards. The effect is as of starched ribbons of lace tatting.

ATHYRIUM

A. filix-femina. (The spelling is critical. *Filix* is a fern, a member of the family Filices; *felix -icis* means 'happy'.)
The lady fern comes from the greater part of the Northern Hemisphere and spreads down into Tropical America. It is called the lady fern because of the delicacy of its structure in comparison with the male ferns, which are so called because they are more robust than the lady fern.

The fronds are lanceolate in shape, bipinnate, but occasionally tripinnate towards the base of the blade. The pinnules are pinnatifid and slenderly pointed. The whole plant has an air of fineness and daintiness. The maximum length of the fronds is about three feet. Deciduous.

The lady fern is easy to grow and a little shade at the middle of the day will suffice so long as the root run is cool and moist. In shady, moist sites many sporelings may occur, and no two are quite the same. It dislikes wind even more than many other ferns.

It is very prone to variations and these fall into groups, but many will be found as clones.

A. f-f. Cristatum group. Variable degrees of flat, fan-shaped cresting on the frond tips and the ends of the pinnae.

A. f-f. Cruciatum group. Pinnae arise in fours, each four from a common point on the rachis. The upper pair of each four tend to overlap the lower pair of the next four up. This is taken to amazing lengths in the next fern.

A. f-f. 'Victoriae', in which the pinnules are reduced to vestiges and the long, ribbon-like pinnae cross perfectly regularly and geometrically. Each pinna terminates in a branched crest. Sporelings do not come true, but the Victoriae group, as distinct from the clone, shows varying degrees of cruciate formation, terminal cresting, and reduction in pinnule size. Reduction of the pinnae themselves is almost *ad absurdum* in the next variety.

A. f-f. 'Frizelliae', the tatting fern. Each pinna is reduced to a structure like a tiny, blown Brussels sprout. About 18 inches.

A. f-f. 'Frizelliae Capitatum' is a named one of several forms in which the fronds are crested, each element of the branched crests having its own, rosary-like frond vestiges.

A. f-f. 'Gemmatum' is a dwarf form for crevices in the rock garden. It has red stems and corymbose terminal crests. Nine inches.

A. f-f. 'Grandiceps' is a heavily crested form of eighteen inches with, nevertheless, a lacy, almost frothy appearance in light green.

A. f-f. 'Minutissimum' is a perfect miniature lady fern, only six inches high, and ideal for the rock garden or a shady tub or trough garden.

A. f-f. 'Vernoniae Cristatum'. A form in which the pinnae are unusually broad, crisped, and daintily crested.

A. f-f. Plumosum group. There are several forms with 'plumosum' in their names, but this is really a group and there has been far too much dishing out of cultivar names. The fronds may be divided as far as being quadripinnate, and tend towards a markedly golden-green colour. The plants are deliciously feathery and dislike wind intensely. Fronds may be three feet long. Various crested forms, many of them unwelcome, bear varietal names.

A. niponicum 'Pictum' (syn. *A. goeringianum* 'Pictum', *A. niponicum metallicum*). The Japanese painted fern
The 'painted' form of the species occurs in 50 per cent of populations in the wild in Japan. The fronds are two feet long, triangular, and the longest pair of pinnae is the second or third, rather than the basal pair. It is pinnate, and the fronds are pointed.

The colouring of this fern is its great attraction. The rachis and pinna midribs are burgundy-pink, while the proximal part of each pinna is dove-grey, with blue and pink tones in it.

It is not fully hardy, but thrives in warm, moist parts of the British Isles and

Above: *Asplenium trichomanes* and *Polypodium interjectum*, wild in an old wall. Sherkin Island, Co. Cork, Ireland. *Nicola Kelly*

Below: Croziers of *Athyrium filix-femina* with *Dryopteris affinis* in the background. Bramble Cottage, Ottery St Mary, Devon. *John Kelly*

Right: *Athyrium filix-femina* 'Frizelliae Capitatum, with *Trillium sessile* in the foreground. King's Gatchell, Ottery St Mary, Devon. *John Kelly*

Below: *Blechnum chilense*. Ilnacullin, Garinish Island, Co. Cork, Ireland. *John Kelly*

only the coldest, driest districts finally defeat it. Even so, it is an asset to any conservatory which does not become too hot, or to a shady spot in the greenhouse. It likes a moist root run but good drainage. Deciduous, but barely so when well suited, continuing fresh until early winter. Good with the small, but broad-leaved bamboo, *Shibataea kumasasa*.

BLECHNUM

B. penna-marina
A good, very small fern for the non-calcareous rock garden. It comes from Australia, Tasmania, New Zealand and South America. It has sterile fronds, which are simply pinnate, very leathery, almost black-green, and up to six inches long. The fertile fronds are a foot long and erect.

It forms dense mats and away from the rock garden is ideal for growing to cover ground among shade- and acid-loving plants and can be grown to great effect on the peat wall. It is not possible in limy soils.

B. p-m. alpina is even smaller, making quite prostrate, tight mats.

B. p-m. cristatum is not very exciting.

B. spicant. The hard fern
This is an elegant fern of simple structure that can be found all over the British Isles on acid formations. It is widespread in Europe and North America. Wherever a near-vertical, dripping bank is found, there you will see the comb-like, simply pinnate sterile fronds, up to two feet long, but mostly in the one foot to eighteen inches range. They are bright, glossy green, very leathery and with several pinnae per inch. The fertile fronds are longer, erect, and with narrowly spiky pinnae, in contrast to the spreading habit of the sterile ones, which tend towards rosette formation.

This fern is highly intolerant of lime. Though I have not found it necessary in practice, I feel bound to advise the use of rainwater or water from another lime-free source in dry spells. Whereas I watered many thousands of lime-hating plants with limy water, even in pots, for many years with no loss of quality, I have only grown this fern in Ireland, where it needs no watering. In moist soils, the hard fern grows in full sun, where it may be reduced in size, so a place in a crevice in the rock garden should suit it perfectly.

B. chilense
There is a great deal of confusion concerning this plant, as it is often distributed

as *B. tabulare*, a name which is also wrongly given to *B. magellanicum*. I am reinforced in the view that these (*B. chilense* and *B. magellanicum*) are distinct species and not synonyms by having examined what I can only take to be colonies of each in the garden of Kells House, in County Kerry, Ireland (but see under *B. magellanicum* below).

B. chilense is a bold fern. In a moist, shaded spot its fronds approach or even exceed three feet long and arch dramatically. The root is rhizomatous, and the mass of individual fronds becomes imposing as it conquers territory. Beside a stream, its very dark green, broad, simply pinnate fronds can be sinister or quietly peaceful by turns.

It is hardy in mild areas of England, Wales and western Scotland, as well as in much of Ireland. It is capable of making a wide colony of jagged, tough, leathery fronds which create a tropical effect. In fact, it is heat-resistant as long as there is a good deal of moisture in the air, and is planted in the Sub-Tropics. It makes a remarkable, if sombre combination with dicksonias.

B. magellanicum

This fern appears to be a one half to two-thirds size edition of *B. chilense*. It is almost always distributed as *B. tabulare*, thus making the blechnum conundrum all the more dense. The true *B. tabulare* arises from a caudex and has a short trunk, unlike the other species, which send up individual fronds from rhizomes.

This may not concern the general gardener all that much, but he should be aware of what might go under what label. *B. magellanicum* is hardier than *B. chilense*, and those looking for the same sort of effect in a colder spot, or for executing it in a small garden, are best advised to write to nurserymen offering *B. tabulare*, asking them about the habit of mature plants of what they are selling. It is lovely with candelabra primulas, meconopsis, and contrasting with Japanese maples. Persistent.

CETERACH

This genus is recently included in *Asplenium*. I have retained the 'old' name in the interests of gardeners, who will find it hard enough to obtain without confusing the nurserymen who still list it thus.

C. officinarum. The rusty-back fern

Northern Hemisphere including Britain. It grows in walls as if they had been made specially for it, and less so in crevices in limestone rocks in the wild than

Blechnum tabulare — the true plant — showing fertile fronds. King's Gatchell, Ottery St Mary, Devon. *John Kelly*

one supposes it must have done at some time in its history. It is a dwarf fern, whose fronds have a uniquely zig-zag appearance due to the pinnae, which are rounded at their ends, yet set on the rachis with flat bases, and are alternate, yet overlapping. It gets its common name because the entire under-surface of the frond becomes brown with sori.

If you can persuade it to establish, it is an intriguing and attractive fern for crevice planting in the rock garden. It is another that is said to need old lime mortar in its soil, but I know of no one who has done a control and grown it without, so am not in a position to advise its omission. It will take quite a lot of sun and has a short-term 'resurrection' quality of returning to green life after being browned-off by drought.

CHEILANTHES. Lip ferns

C. distans

New Zealand. This is a fern that is unusually well adapted for dry conditions. It is an alpine, and grows in nature on stony hillsides where it may receive full sun and be subject to periods of drought. However, it always has a cool, moist root run, and should be provided with this in cultivation.

It is hardy, but susceptible to wet in winter as so many alpine flowering plants are, most especially many New Zealanders. The usual advice given is to grow it in an alpine house, but how many of us own such structures? A vertical crevice in the rock garden, preferably overhung by a rock, is probably the best bet.

The frond is a foot or less long, with a wiry stem and rachis. It is pinnate, the opposite pairs of pinnae short, saggitate in outline and pinnatifid. They are unusually widely separated so that the spaces between the pairs are approximately equal to the spaces occupied by them. Many species in the genus are covered in a waxy, powdery bloom, but this one is intensely hairy.

Two other species, *C. farinosa* and *C. myriophylla*, are occasionally offered. The former, from the Himalaya, is powdery; the latter, from the Tropics, has much-divided fronds. Neither appears likely to be growable in the open garden.

CRYPTOGRAMMA

C. crispa. The parsley fern

The triangular, tripinnate or even quadripinnate fronds of this dwarf fern look just like the non-curly kind of parsley, or like the curly kind does when it is very young. It has separate fertile fronds, which are tripinnate with linear pinnules, rather like the leaflet arrangement in some artemisia species.

It is a devoted hater of lime and demands good drainage. The peat wall is a good place for it so long as it has its own pocket of leafy, gravelly soil. Alternatively it is probably best suited in a shady, deep crevice in a rock garden or retaining wall. A combination that would be fascinating, and which I have not, alas, tried, would be with *Corydalis cashmeriana*, whose foliage is almost a blue grey version of the fern's, and whose sapphire-like flowers glow in shady places.

CYATHEA

This is a genus of tree ferns from the Andes and New Zealand. One or two species are established in south-western Ireland, but they are of more general immediate interest as designers of gardens in large cities are now using them successfully, owing to the mildness of metropolitan climates.

C. dealbata

This is the most usual one. It is not very tall, and specimens with three-foot

The Japanese holly fern, *Cyrtomium falcatum*. King's Gatchell, Ottery St Mary, Devon. *John Kelly*

trunks are quite mature. The trunks are more slender than in dicksonias, and the fronds are bi- or tripinnate and white beneath. Grown in containers, these tree ferns can become pot bound and not suffer, so they are not difficult to move around. However, they need abundant moisture and shade, and in hot weather the trunks should be sprayed at least once a day with water that is not too cold.

C. australis
This one is larger, and can reach ten feet in height. It can be grown out of doors from May to October in most places, but then needs to be brought into a conservatory capable of accommodating its eight-foot frond span.

CYRTOMIUM

C. falcatum. The Japanese holly fern
Currently there is a move to re-classify this as *Phanerophlebia falcata*, and it will be found listed under that name in works which are too useful to be ignored

when you are trying to find what nursery stocks which plants.

The range of the species is from Japan to Hawaii and Indo-China, and thus embraces many climates. Some forms are hardier than others, but good results may be expected away from eastern counties of England and Scotland.

The pinnate fronds are dark, glossy green, making a fine contrast to other ferns. It prefers a northern aspect – full shade, in other words. On the whole it is hardier than generally supposed and may be destined to become more widely grown. Those with more markedly toothed pinnae, such as *C.f.* 'Rochfordianum', are said to be the hardiest.

CYSTOPTERIS. The bladder ferns

C. bulbifera
North America. This is a widely variable fern, whose fronds, according to conditions, can be anything from under a foot long to more than three but are usually around thirty inches in length. It can, when well suited, spread rapidly by means of the numerous bulbils which drop from the rachis and quickly root.

The frond is triangular, bipinnate and ochre-green. It is said to prefer a calcareous soil, but in any event should be given plenty of room among shrubs or at the edge of light woodland. It is deciduous.

C. dickeana
Although this is a rare plant in Britain, confined to one or two stations in Scotland, it is easy to grow and propagate. It is only two or three inches high, pinnate, and with a congested appearance because of the overlapping of the pinnae.

It is a treasure for the small rock garden, a most attractive miniature fern, and wonderfully so when it unfurls in spring, when a mature plant looks like a head of tight curls. Deciduous.

C. fragilis. Brittle bladder fern
This is quite a common species in the highland parts of the British Isles, where it favours crevices in rocks. The frond is from three to eighteen inches long, tripinnate, triangular-lanceolate, with the pinnae divided into rounded, but slender lobes. It is light green and completely deciduous.

It makes quite a wide mat for a small fern, although it is perfectly well behaved. The rock garden is the best place for it, where it can be grown in a flat or gently sloping pocket where the soil has been made stony but rich at the same time.

Davallia mariesii. Clodagh, Sherkin Island, Co. Cork, Ireland. *Nicola Kelly*

C. montana. Mountain bladder fern
The habit of this fern is totally different, as it has a rhizomatous root from which individual fronds arise, instead of a mass of caudices. It prefers lime in cultivation and occurs on limestone rocks in the wild. It is occasionally offered and would be most likely to succeed in a shady corner of a limestone rock garden or retaining wall.
Also offered on occasion is *C. regia*, which Reginald Kaye praises for its much-divided, emerald-green fronds that are only six inches high.

DAVALLIA

D. mariesii. The hare's foot fern
Japan, China, Korea. This most attractive fern is increasingly recognised as being hardy away from the colder areas. Other species, such as *D. trichomanoides* and *D. pyxidata*, are only suitable for the cool greenhouse or conservatory, but the hare's foot fern deserves a choice spot outside or, at the least, a long turn out of doors in a container.

The vernacular name comes from the appearance of the rootstock, which is an iris-like tangle of rhizomes, covered with scales that look like thin fur. Each growing branch end looks something like the foot of a small hare. The fronds are produced individually and are triangular, on stems of the same length as the blades. They are tripinnate and beautifully filigreed. Deciduous.

In the open garden a sheltered, shady, well-drained spot should be chosen next to a moist, mossy rock over which the rhizomes can spread. In a large container in company with other plants it can be allowed to overwinter outside, but in a smaller pot it should be brought indoors for the winter.

DENNSTAEDTIA

D. punctilobula. Hay-scented fern
North America. This pretty fern has a reputation for being highly invasive, but this is by no means universally observed. It is in fact incredibly tough and puts up with all kinds of adverse conditions. In a highly congenial position it colonises ground rapidly by means of underground runners, but in the mixed border it is usually quite well behaved.

Its fronds are from one foot to two-and-a-half feet high, tripinnate, with each pinnule deeply and gracefully cut. There seems to be a form that is not much more than nine inches high, which spreads enthusiastically but prettily. It is deciduous. A crested variety is known.

An excellent companion for this fern is a colony of *Meconopsis grandis*.

DICKSONIA

D. antarctica
Australia, Tasmania. I know of no more exciting sight in gardening than a grove of mature specimens of this noble tree fern. Its trunks, almost two feet thick in century-old trees, are as if petrified, and the combination of a stand of these, topped by their huge filigree umbrellas of fronds, touching to form a diamond-studded ceiling, stops time dead in its tracks, for these are the botanical equivalent of living dinosaurs.

The fronds are six feet long, bipinnate, almost tripinnate, and sharply leathery. Thirty fronds a year may be produced by the crown of a mature specimen, and these arise as bold croziers from the centres, often being initiated as late as well into August.

They require a mild, moist climate and grow beautifully and 'seed' themselves in much of Cornwall, several districts in Devon, and have survived several

Above: *Dennstaedtia punctilobula*. The young plants of *Meconopsis grandis* flower towards midsummer. King's Gatchell, Ottery St Mary, Devon. *John Kelly*

Below: *Dicksonia antarctica*. Kells House, Co. Kerry, Ireland. *John Kelly*

winters on the Dorset coast. There are niches in South Wales where they succeed, and they can be spectacular in western Scotland, as at Logan Botanic Garden, by Stranraer, where they are lawn specimens. In Ireland they are unsurpassed, growing well at Mount Usher and other Irish Sea coast gardens and coming into their own in Kerry, where they are utterly majestic.

In containers they are very fine for city gardens. When they get too big the trunks can be cut through and the tops replanted, as they are, in fact, solid, mixed masses of old and young, functioning roots.

D. fibrosa
This species comes from New Zealand. It is said not to be as strong a grower, but information given to me by designers specialising in London gardens leads to the conclusion that it is hardier than *D. antarctica* and that its less robust growth may be no bad thing for their purposes.

D. squarrosa
This has a slender, black trunk, like a bundle of high-voltage cables when young. The fronds are very wide and long and of more open structure than in the other species. It sometimes runs underground and produces new plants. Possible outside probably only in south-western Ireland.

It is advisable to spray the trunks of tree ferns during hot, dry weather. This is not necessary or practicable where several specimens are growing out of doors in the sort of climatic conditions that suit them, but tree ferns in containers, or growing in cities or places that can became hot and dry, may suffer unless it is done.

DRYOPTERIS

D. affinis. The golden-scaled male fern
This is the fern that most of us have known until recently as *D. borreri*, and which is sometimes known as *D. pseudomas*. It is widely spread in Europe and the British Isles. It is often thought to be extremely closely related to the common male fern, *D. filix-mas*, but in fact is not. Visually the main differences are the golden scales on the long stems, which are most noticeable with the sun behind them, and the neatly squared-off pinnae, which are not irregularly rounded. It is also semi-persistent, whereas *D. filix-mas* is deciduous.

The fronds are lanceolate, usually about three feet long, glossy and leathery, tending sometimes towards an ochre green, at others to deep green. They are pinnate, the pinnae deeply pinnatifid, adjoining pinna edges parallel and close

Above: *Dryopteris affinis* 'Cristata The King'. King's Gatchell, Ottery St Mary, Devon, *John Kelly*

Below: *Dryopteris affinis* 'Cristata Angustata'. King's Gatchell, Ottery St Mary, Devon. *John Kelly*

together, the tips square. The overall effect is one of regularity and neatness.

It is easy to grow, preferring dappled shade but taking a good deal of sun if the soil is moist. Happiest, perhaps, without lime, but reasonably lime-tolerant on the whole. There is virtually no situation in a mixed border where this plant is not welcome, and it is the one that I would plant near camellias, as its neat fronds match and complement the formality of camellia foliage.

D.a. Congesta group. Plants usually no more than a foot high, with overlapping pinnae.

D.a. 'Congesta Cristata'. Properly a group. Fronds are, as you might expect, congested and crested to varying extents.

D.a. Cristata group. Plants with terminal crests, about two feet high, almost persistent.

D.a. 'Cristata The King'. A superlative fern, perhaps the one to grow if you can only have one. The fronds are three feet long, each with a neatly handsome terminal crest, and each pinna terminates in a crest. All the crests are evenly matched, so that the essential character of the species is not lost, but if anything enhanced.

D.a. 'Cristata Angustata'. Like a very slim version of the above.

D.a. 'Grandiceps Askew'. Fronds two feet long, the margins crisped. The main feature is a very heavy terminal crest. Likely to be expensive.

D.a. polydactyla. The name given to a putatively wild-occurring form with many-fingered terminal crests on apex and pinnae. Not very attractive.

D.a. 'Stableri'. A foot taller than usual, with short pinnae making the fronds narrow. There is, apparently, a wavy-fronded form of this, but it sounds undistinguished.

D. carthusiana. Narrow buckler fern
Northern Hemisphere, including the British Isles. It is like a smaller and narrower version of the broad buckler fern, *Dryopteris dilatata*, and is not often grown in gardens, preferring a marshy spot. It is mentioned here because it is occasionally offered for sale. The specific epithet is strange. It seems to mean 'In honour of Chartreuse', whereas if it were 'of the Carthusians' it would be *carthusianorum*.

D. dilatata. Broad buckler fern
Northern Hemisphere, common in the British Isles. The fronds are tripinnate,

anything from two to four feet long and broadly triangular. The bases of the fronds are very wide and the width reduces so sharply towards the tips that the curvature of the frond edge is often reversed. It is found on acid formations in moist, leafy soil in shady situations in the wild. Deciduous.

This attractive fern is not as easy to grow as some would have you believe. It hates any hint of drought but also demands very good drainage. When happy it is a very 'ferny' plant, just what one imagines a woodland fern should be. In fact it is best planted in acid woodland and in company, but not inside the circle of branch tips of shallow-rooted trees. It is a good waterside fern so long as there is not too much sun.

D.d. 'Crispa Whiteside'. Smaller than the species with crisped, wavy fronds up to two feet long.

D.d. 'Grandiceps'. The pinnae are crested, and the fronds end in dense, ball-like, corymbose crests.

D.d. 'Lepidota Cristata'. A two-foot plant with a very lacy appearance due to the finely cut pinnules. There is also a degree of cresting.

D. erythrosora
Temperate East Asia. The frond formation is reminiscent of the European male fern, but it is a smaller plant of about two feet in height. It is deciduous, and the new fronds are coppery pink until mature, when they turn green. The frond is almost tripinnate. The red colouring appears again in the indusia, which are bright red and give rise to the epithet *erythrosora*.

Its deciduousness is marginal, as the fronds last well into the winter and longer in mild areas, but it would be misleading to deem it semi-persistent. It is lovely with *Photinia* 'Red Robin', whose new growths are of the same sort of colour but more so, pieris, and *Heuchera* 'Palace Purple', which is not really purple at all, but mahogany-maroon. A fern for the mixed border.

D. filix-mas. Common male fern
Northern Hemisphere, common in the British Isles, rare in North America. It is extremely easy to grow this fern, which will succeed in almost any situation where there is a modicum of good soil. If your garden is not ideal for ferns, with a shallow soil, for instance, then you can try this one. On the whole, though, the plain species is not a plant for those who like elegance and quality, and it can sow itself rather too successfully. There are, however, some better-behaved and interesting varieties.

Right: Young fronds of *Dryopteris erythrosora*. King's Gatchell, Ottery St Mary, Devon. *John Kelly*

Below: Dryopteris filix-mas. Abbotsbury Gardens, Dorset. *John Kelly*

The species is robust, with fronds up to five feet long. They are lanceolate and pinnate with deeply pinnatifid pinnae. The pinnules are irregular, rounded at the tips, and look as though they do not 'fit together' properly. Alongside *D. affinis* the plant looks decidedly coarse.

D.f-m. barnesii appears to be a natural variety and not a cultivar, as it comes completely true from spores. Its fronds are narrower, as the pinnae are shorter and distinctly arching. The pinnae are also serrated along the margins. It is up to four feet high.

D.f-m. 'Crispa' seems to be a dwarf clone, not much more than a foot tall and with crisped pinnae. It is an easy-going plant for the rock garden.

D.f-m 'Crispa Crispata' comes true from spores. It is two or three inches taller than the preceding variety, also crisped, but with neat crests.

D.f-m. Cristata group consists of sporelings of varying degrees of cresting.

D.f-m 'Jackson' is an outstanding crested clone with solid, curved, corymbose crests at the frond apices and pinnae. Some think it freakish.

D.f-m. 'Martindale'. Another cultivar that comes true from spores. The pinnae are crested, and curve upwards towards the frond apex, becoming closer together as the frond narrows. This has been termed a 'fishtail' effect, and with justification.

Among other forms that are available from time to time are: those of the Polydactyla group, in which the frond apices and pinna tips have long, finger-like crests (not everyone's cup of tea); 'Depauperata', with ribbon-like pinnae; 'Linearis', which also has reduced pinnae, and various crested forms of 'Linearis'.

D. goldiana. The giant wood fern
North America. This is not really a giant, as its maximum height is around four feet, but it is nevertheless imposing. The frond is ovate-lanceolate, narrow at the base, pinnate, the pinnae pinnatifid.

It is deciduous and is most attractive when unfurling. It likes the same sort of conditions as *D. dilatata*. It is occasionally offered for sale.

D. marginalis
Another North American, known as the marginal buckler fern. It is occasionally commercially available and worth obtaining, as its fronds have a blue tinge that

is not all that common in ferns. It is persistent and tough, liking a good, leafy, well-drained soil.

GYMNOCARPIUM

G. dryopteris. The oak fern
Europe, northern Britain. This fern has had so many Latin names — no fewer than seven — that one can have little faith in its retaining the present one for long. It is a rhizomatous species, with individual, nine-inch, wiry, black stems, each of which carries its blade aloft like a triangular umbrella. The two lowest pinnae are large and tripinnate, while the rest are progressively smaller and bipinnate. It is a byword for elegance and daintiness among ferns, and its soft green fronds cannot be confused with anything other than the next species. It should, however, be remembered that the American oak fern is *Onoclea sensibilis* (q.v.). It is deciduous.

It loves to wander gently in a peat wall, a shady part of the rock garden, or just in a moist, peaty, shaded niche in the mixed border.

G. robertianum. The limestone polypody
Europe, North America, northern England, Wales. Its vernacular name made more sense when it was classified as a polypodium species, but it is a denizen of limestone pavements and screes, where it grows in sunny situations but obtains part shade from the surrounding scree stones or by growing in crevices. It is a little like the oak fern, but not all that much, being less broadly triangular. However, it is similar in that the frond seems to be divided into three lobes; in fact it is not branched, but the lowest pinnae are tripinnate, while the rest are bipinnate. Deciduous.

The limestone polypody is not difficult to grow, but its rhizome should be among stones and not covered with soil. A similar environment to that liked by *Adiantum pedatum* is fairly ideal. It is about fifteen inches tall, so fit for the larger rock garden, where it looks more at home than in a border.

HYMENOPHYLLUM

To mention ferns in this genus and *Trichomanes speciosum* is to introduce plants that are difficult for ordinary gardeners to obtain and even more difficult to grow. However, an account of the ferns that grow in gardens would be inadequate without their inclusion.

These are the filmy ferns. Their fronds are in most cases only a cell or two thick and they will only grow where the air is constantly full of finely-divided water drops or 100 per cent humid. Like *Eritrichium nanum*, vegetable sheep, and some desperately tricky tropical plants, they belong among the greatest challenges cultivators can face. The wardian case is the best place for them. I include them because they are, in fact, grown, and may come the way of anyone consorting with fellow fern-enthusiasts.

H. tunbridgense
Almost unbelievably, this fern has its classic site in Tunbridge Wells, Kent. What is left of it in the wild is in the west of Scotland. It looks like a much-branched, filmy seaweed. It has pinnate fronds, each pinna dividing into two or three equal parts with black midribs showing starkly against the translucent, green material of the blade.

H. wilsonii
This occurs in western Great Britain. It is even more filmy than the foregoing, but can be kept going in leafmould in a wardian case, where it welcomes the occasional spraying.

The Killarney fern, another filmy fern, is *Trichomanes speciosum*. It grows in County Kerry in deep, rocky stream gorges into which the sun does not penetrate and where ferns of all kinds grow with a pushy, tumid urge that has to be seen to be believed. It is possibly in some ways the greatest wonder of the flora of these islands. It has been damaged in the past, but luckily some of its sites are under closely concerned private stewardship.

HYPOLEPIS

H. millefolium
New Zealand. This is a delightfully attractive, fairly small fern which, unfortunately, can only be grown in the mildest areas. It is rather invasive, but those who grow it tend to make room for it, as it is a truly beautiful rarity. The fronds are about a foot high, of a sage green colour that has emerald at its heart, and exquisitely tripinnate. It likes not so much a soil as a deep deposit of old fallen leaves, where the underlying formation, whether acidic or calcareous, will be of little concern.

MATTEUCCIA

M. struthiopteris. The shuttlecock fern
Northern Hemisphere. Also known as the ostrich-feather fern. This is one of

Matteuccia struthiopteris. University of Leiden Botanic Garden, Holland.

the easiest of all ferns to grow, but is sometimes not that simple to establish. It is completely deciduous and sometimes fails to reappear after the third or fourth winter of its life. However, I have a suspicion that in some cases it is subject to crown damage during gardening operations.

In spring the fronds uncurl in the most delectable manner, forming as they do so the most perfect shuttlecock. The plant runs when established, but never in a bumptious way. Indeed, a wide drift of this fern, such as the one that can be seen in Holland by a pond at the University of Leiden's Botanic Garden, is a superb sight with each individual shuttlecock showing off its formation. Other ferns have something of the shuttlecock conformation but tend to grow in tight clumps so that, as we have said elsewhere, it is aesthetically a good idea to divide and separate them.

Ideally, a marshy, or at least a moist site should be chosen, but this accommodating fern will grow perfectly happily in the most ordinary garden conditions. However, the soil must not be heavy and sticky or of any kind that cracks if it becomes dry, as this will kill the plant. It should not dry out at all, but a liberal application of organic matter should go a long way towards preventing that.

The fronds can be as little as two feet tall in such a situation, or as much as five in moisture and shade. They are of two kinds, sterile and fertile, and it is the sterile ones that give the plant its familiar appearance. They are pinnate, with pinnatifid pinnae, and sharply oblanceolate. (The prefix ob- indicates a fern frond or a leaf that is broadest in its distal part narrowing throughout the proximal portion; obovate is another example. Oblong and obtuse are, of course, quite different.) The fertile fronds are much shorter than the sterile ones, which is an unusual feature, as in most dimorphic ferns they are longer and conspicuous.

M. orientalis
This is quite different and has sterile fronds that arch right over. In *M. struthiopteris* the stems of the fronds are reduced to very little, the pinnae of the blades reaching almost to ground level as they become shorter and shorter. This is what in fact makes the shuttlecock effect so striking. In *M. orientalis*, the stems are much longer, occupying about one third of the total frond length. This combines with the falling-over-backwards arching to present a most un-shuttlecock appearance, especially as the fertile fronds are quite erect and long. Plants are sometimes offered under this name, and if they are true to name they represent a very fine species, but not a shuttlecock fern. Plants with the shuttlecock shape, particularly with pinnae reaching right down the fronds, are misnamed and belong to *M. struthiopteris*.

ONOCLEA

O. sensibilis. American oak fern. Sensitive fern
This is a hardy, tough fern, dubbed sensitive because its fronds disappear at the first hint of frost. They arise from a wandering rhizome and are dimorphic. The fertile ones are usually just over a foot high, half of which is stem. The blades are triangular, and the degree of pinnateness decreases as the apex is approached, so that the lower part is cut to the rachis, at mid-frond the cut stops short of it, and towards the tip the cutting is shallow. This makes the frond look as though it consists of oak leaves mounted on a central ribbon which widens as they grow shorter. The oak-leaf effect is given by the sinuate leaf margins.

This is a fern that has been accused of being invasive, but I have not found it so. Like any other with a creeping rhizome, it is designed to make widening mats of roots just below soil level, and it should be planted with that in mind

and not castigated for following its nature. It is certainly no garden thug, but a pretty decoration for the skirts of shrubs or for accompanying primulas, meconopsis, and other damp-loving plants near water or in a moist, dapple-shaded border.

OREOPTERIS

O. limbosperma (syn. *Thelypteris limbosperma*)
Europe, including the British Isles, North America. The mountain, or lemon-scented fern, is conspicuous because of its bright, yellow-green colour, and is easily distinguished from male ferns, which it resembles, by the lemon scent of the fronds when crushed.

It grows from an underground, creeping rhizome and delights in moist, acid soils; it will not tolerate lime. Deciduous.

OSMUNDA. The royal fern

O. regalis
The distribution of the royal fern is extremely wide. It extends throughout Europe and North and South America, and occurs in Africa and India. In North America it meets other species with more limited distributions. In the British Isles it varies from rare in England to abundant in south-western Ireland, where it is common on roadside banks and old, boggy fields.

It is anything from two to five feet tall in gardens, sometimes more. In Ireland it is commonplace to find it ten feet tall in bogs in full sun (such as it is). It is dimorphic, the sterile fronds broad and strikingly bipinnate. The fertile fronds rise above the centre of the plant and are russet in colour and shaped like the flower heads of astilbes.

It is a lover of wet places and peaty, leafy soils and is magnificent by water, making a stately presence with gunneras and lysichitums. It will grow perfectly well, however, in any good garden soil that does not dry out, but its size will reflect its degree of comfort. In autumn the fronds turn gold before falling for the winter. It does not like lime.

O.r. 'Crispa' has pinnules which, instead of being smooth, are uniformly undulating.

O.r. 'Cristata group' plants have crests at the ends of the fronds, pinnae and pinnules. It is slow growing compared with the type.

Osmunda regalis. Wild, near Dunmanway. Co. Cork, Ireland. *Nicola Kelly*

Paesia scaberula. Kells House, Co. Kerry, Ireland. *John Kelly*

O.r. 'Purpurascens' starts out with coppery pink fronds in spring, but these change to green, leaving the stems and rachis purple.

O. cinnamomea
This species is confined to North America. It is never as tall in gardens as in the wild, making a plant of about three feet. While not as spectacular as *O. regalis*, it is not a lime hater and is a plant for those who cannot grow its larger relative. However, it still requires a good, deep, moist soil and should not be attempted on shallow soils over chalk.

The common name of cinnamon fern derives from the hairs on the fronds, which are white when they unfurl but then change to a rusty cinnamon colour, a deeper version of which occurs in the fertile fronds.

O. claytonia
This is the interrupted fern, so called because the fertile fronds have groups of normal-shaped, sterile pinnae alternating with groups of fertile ones. The fern has a more open structure than *O. regalis* and is not as attractive, although it is most handsome when well suited. Unfortunately, it is a little fussy, and must have shade as well as moisture, and no lime.

Osmundas are not easy to propagate. The spores must be sown as soon as ripe, as their viability is measured in times less than a week. It is not always easy to determine their ripeness. In *O. cinnamomea* the sporangia turn from green to cinnamon when ripe, but the spores are green. In *O. regalis* the sporangia are brown before they are ripe, and the spores are green. In *O. claytonia* the sporangia turn black when ripe, but the spores themselves are green. They tend to resent being disturbed, so division has to be undertaken with care. This is not that easy, because a trunk-like caudex, which may be up to nine inches tall, can be formed, and the roots consist of large, matted masses of fibres. These are the osmunda fibres of orchid growers and florists, and it is unfortunately true that the destruction of many stands of fine osmundas in the wild is directly due to the collection of this fibre. It is difficult to understand why environmentalists, often eager to attack on other fronts, sometimes with inadequate research, have not acted on behalf of these beleaguered ferns, many of whose British locations have been laid waste.

PAESIA

P. scaberula
This is a genus of alpine ferns from New Zealand, of which there are about a

Phymatosorus scolopendria on an evergreen oak. Kells House, Co. Kerry, Ireland.
John Kelly

dozen. I had not imagined any to be in cultivation in the British Isles, but it is offered for sale by one or two nurseries, and I have seen a very fine, well-established, vigorous stand of it in County Kerry, Ireland, where it grows in the open in the dappled shade of an evergreen oak. It is also reported to be succeeding in the open in one or two gardens in Great Britain.

It is about eighteen inches high, the tri- to quadripinnate fronds growing from a creeping rhizome and making a colony six feet or more across. The delicate tracery of the fronds is most beautiful. In New Zealand it grows in full sun in stony, alpine-type soils, but a good soil and part shade seem called for in the garden. It is said to be invasive, but one would need to define one's terms. It could well be hardier than it is at present thought to be, and spores from provenances promising resistance to frost would be most desirable.

PHEGOPTERIS

P. connectilis. The beech fern
Europe, including northern Britain, Asia, North America. Yet another species

has been batted about among botanists as its names have changed in bewildering fashion. Most recently it was *Thelypteris phegopteris*.

It is a dainty fern, nine to eighteen inches high, with triangular-ovate fronds arising from a creeping, slender, underground rhizome. The fronds are pinnate, the pinnae deeply pinnatifid. It is distinguished from the oak fern, *Gymnocarpium dryopteris*, by the overall shape of the frond (it is much more narrowly triangular), by that of the pinna (lanceolate, as opposed to oblong-lanceolate) and by the white hairs that grow all over the fronds.

The beech fern is very keen on a damp spot and does not like lime. It is a good plant for the shady part of the rock garden, where its rhizomes will run into crevices as well as colonise flat areas of soil. It looks well grown at the front of a shady border with hellebores, meconopsis, primulas, *Hydrangea quercifolia*, and other woodlanders, and it is ideal for the peat wall.

PHYMATOSORUS

P. scolopendria

Countries bordering the Indian Ocean. Of all the ferns that can be grown out of doors in Britain, this is the most reminiscent of the flora of the Sub-Tropics, especially when growing epiphytically.

The rhizome is slender and does not need to be in soil at all, as it acts primarily as an anchor for the fronds, rather after the manner of bromeliads. The plant seeks similar places, too, and is as happy on the shady side of a stone wall as anywhere. Note, though, that the wall need not be of the retaining kind. In cultivation the rhizome may be artificially attached to the wall, or to the branch of a tree, just as one would attach tillandsias, vriesias, or aechmas.

The fronds are of two kinds, simple and pinnatifid. The simple ones are linear-lanceolate. The pinnatifid fronds are reminiscent of the American scarlet oak, but on a larger scale, with broad sinuses between the pinnae. It is a simplified version of the fronds of many polypodiums, and indeed the species was included in that genus for many years. In the wild the fronds can be very large, but those in cultivation are under a foot long.

The large, round, chocolate-coloured sori show up beautifully from either side of the translucent frond. They lie in pits on the under-surfaces of both kinds of fronds and are embossed upon the upper ones.

I include this lovely fern, even though it is not currently available commercially, because it is hardy in south-western England, western Scotland, and the south of Ireland. It is little known and deserves to be tried wherever the climate is sufficiently mild and above all moist. Propagation is child's play: the mere

Polypodium australe 'Wilharris'. King's Gatchell, Ottery St Mary, Devon. *John Kelly*

detaching of a section of root and attaching it again somewhere else is all that is necessary.

POLYPODIUM

The common polypody of the British Isles, which also occurs in Europe, Asia, the Azores and the Canaries, has hitherto been regarded as one species, *P. vulgare*, showing a wide variation.

It is now considered to represent three species, *P. australe*, from the British and Atlantic Islands, with *P. a.* subspecies *azoricum* confined to the Azores and Canaries; *P. interjectum*, which appears to favour limestone rocks near the sea; and *P. vulgare* itself. They are known as the southern, intermediate, and common polypodies respectively.

P. australe

This fern has pinnatifid fronds, eight to eighteen inches long by three to six inches broad. The sori are oval and chocolate brown. It tolerates very dry conditions and is in fact the species that grows on the smithy roof at Abbotsbury, Dorset (see p. 21). However, in that particular case I have reason to suspect that the plants there and elsewhere at Abbotsbury may well belong to the subspecies *azoricum*, as the nearby Sub-Tropical Gardens contain many plants from the Atlantic Islands, including great rarities. This would all the more account for their toleration of drought and exposure, as it is a known characteristic of the subspecies.

P. interjectum
This has fronds that are smaller than the previous species and larger and broader than the next. The sori are yellow and round. The fronds tend to be more grey-green than in either of the other species. Plants I take to be of this species grow on Sherkin Island, Co. Cork, where they huddle among stones and on old walls, keeping out of the ferocious Atlantic gales. It is said to prefer a moister position than the other two species, but I believe its true preference is for a good, rich soil, so long as it is stony.

P. vulgare
The third species requires a moister position than the southern polypody, although it thrives wherever it can root among old, leafy soil. It is epiphytic in mild areas, making tropical-looking clumps in the forks of trees, particularly oak. It will grow beautifully in retaining walls. Its fronds are from three inches to fourteen long and up to two inches wide. The sori are round and yellow.

The nomenclature of the varieties is now complicated. The best way of approaching it is as follows: plants previously known as *P. vulgare cambricum* now belong under *P. australe. P. interjectum* has no varieties so far as I know. Other varieties previously known under *P. vulgare* remain there.

P.a. 'Barrowii'. This is a plumose form in which the pinnae are so deeply cut as to be almost pinnate. They are narrow-based and overlap. The frond texture is thin and the whole plant has a 'leafy' look.The pinnae are long and pointed.

P.a. 'Wilharris' is rare, but occasionally obtainable. The frond tips are crisped and frilled.

P.v. Cristatum group includes crested forms in which the frond apex and pinnae have crests made up of many finger-like filaments. Named among them is 'Forster', which is smaller and neater than most.

P.v. 'Cornubiense' is a strange plant, whose fronds can be normal, tripinnate,

Polystichum setiferum 'Pulcherrimum'. University Botanic Garden, Cambridge. *John Kelly*

or even quadripinnate, but it is difficult to be precise, as they are so finely cut. The fronds are unusually long. Growers usually remove the normal fronds.

P.v. 'Semilacerum' is an attractive variation. The lower pinnae on each frond are deeply pinnatifid at their middles, and the pinnules are long, becoming longest at the middle of the pinnatifid section. Forms called 'Semilacerum Jubilee' and 'Semilacerum Falcatum O'Kelly' are offered, but I do wish the latter name could be rendered down to something less ridiculous.

There are several other named varieties, the names referring to various crested, crisped, and otherwise decorated fronds. A putative hybrid of *P. interjectum, P.* × *mantoniae*, is said to be as much as two feet tall.

POLYSTICHUM

P. aculeatum. The hard shield fern
Europe, including the British Isles. The shield ferns are so called because of

the indusia, which are shield-shaped. *P. aculeatum* is called the hard shield fern in contrast to *P. setiferum*, the soft shield fern. These descriptive terms refer to the textures of the fronds. In general they are reasonably accurate, but it is not always a good idea to rely on such broad differences. 'Aculeatum' means 'prickly', and 'setiferum' means 'bristly', so not much information can be obtained from that!

However, it is in the many variations that most mistakes have been made in the past, and chromosome technology has enabled us to put them right. In *P. setiferum* 2n = 82, while in *P. aculeatum* 2n = 164. This has established the beautiful cultivar 'Pulcherrimum Bevis' as belonging to *P. setiferum*, whereas it had always been thought of as a variation of the other species.

P. aculeatum is a strongly growing plant with three-foot, leathery fronds of deep, glossy green. The frond is pinnate and the pinnae are deeply pinnatifid. Each pinnule is shaped something like the open palm of a mitten with the thumb stuck out (but not nearly as graphically as in *P. setiferum*) and is tipped with a slender but stiff bristle (prickle). Persistent.

It is one of the most beautiful ferns for gardens and is a woodlander by choice, preferring shaded rocks. It is a bold addition to a retaining wall and can act as a strong accent in the shady rock garden. It is not generally happy in the mixed border. *P. aculeatum* enjoys a leafy soil but prefers it to be stony. A soil with too much peat in it is not suitable for this fern, which grows on limestone rocks in nature.

There used to be several varieties that were rightly ascribed to this species, but apart for 'Grandiceps', which is in fact a group of crested forms from spores, none of them appear to be in cultivation, unless tucked away in the hands of specialists.

P. acrostichoides. Christmas fern
North America. The large (three-foot) frond of this unusual fern is pinnate. The pinnae are of two types, the fertile ones occupying the apical portions of the fronds, while the sterile ones are below. The frond is leathery, lanceolate, and covered with white scales when it is very young. The species is persistent and is cut for decoration at Christmas in America.

It is surprisingly uncommon in gardens, but can be obtained commercially. It is easy to grow in a shady spot with plenty of leafmould and does not mind lime. Bipinnate and crested forms are known to specialists, but they do not appear to be widely circulated.

P. andersonii
Another North American species that occasionally finds its way into nursery

lists. The pinnate fronds are holly-like and narrow and from two to three feet long.

P. braunii
This has a wider distribution, occurring in Europe, North America and Asia. It is a non-persistent species, but hardy, and enjoys moist, woodland conditions where it can attain its three-foot frond length. It is bipinnate and glossy, like *P. polyblepharum*, with which is it frequently confused, even among specialist nurserymen.

P. lonchitis The holly fern
Northern Hemisphere, including the British Isles. The holly fern does not look much like holly at all, but its stiff, shiny fronds are pinnate and the simple pinnae have scratchy (that is, not what you would call sharp) points. The fronds are up to two feet long, persistent, and bright green when young, showing up well against the deep green of the older fronds.

The holly fern is not easy to grow, but the best chance is in a deep, leafy crevice in the shaded part of the rock garden.

P. munitum. Sword fern
North America. A species that has been cultivated for many years in the British Isles without ever becoming popular. It is pinnate, rather similar to *P. acrostichoides*, and easily grown, not minding sun. The forms offered for sale are usually quite unlike the normal species, having deeply incised pinnae.

P. polyblepharum
Japan, Korea, China. The specific epithet means 'many-eyelashed' and refers to the soft bristles at the tips of the pinnules. This is a handsome, glossy fern that thrives in deep shade and requires shelter when grown away from the west and south of the British Isles. It is a fine fern for a conservatory border beneath taller, flowering plants.

The slightly leathery fronds are pinnate, the pinnae deeply pinnatifid. The pinnae bear the polystichum 'signature' of the extended mitten.

P. setiferum. The soft shield fern
Europe, including the British Isles. Of all the ferns that can be grown in British gardens this is the easiest and the most accommodating. It will tolerate a good deal of drought, succeeds in poor soils, and is extremely long lived. Its graceful, three to five-foot long fronds are an asset anywhere in the garden – among shrubs, in the mixed border, and even those silly, ridiculously narrow borders

Polystichum setiferum 'Acutilobum' with *Vaccinium glauco-album*. King's Gatchell, Ottery St Mary, Devon. *John Kelly*

between the house wall and the drive that so many of us have had wished on them will support this delightful fern and become features instead of embarrassments.

The fronds are persistent and rise from a tough rootstock, much of which is above ground as branched crowns. They are not leathery and are faintly velvety to the touch. The pinnules are even more markedly mitten-like than in other species, with the 'thumb' quite broad and well-developed. The thumb and the tip of the mitten have terminal whiskers and there may be one or two more at the margin of each pinnule.

The species itself is not often seen in private gardens, its place being taken by the many varieties. In large, public gardens, however, the species may frequently be seen.

In accounting for the following varieties I have sought as far as possible to be up to date with both their naming and availability. However, knowledge advances, and a year may see name changes, the reappearance of 'lost' varieties, and the temporary disappearance of others while they are withdrawn for propagation. Furthermore, it is an area of considerable difficulty, in which it is all too common to find totally different plants under the same label, others with varietal names that belong to utterly different plants, and still others with names that look and sound plausible but have nothing to do with reality.

P.s. Acutilobum group are plants with much narrower fronds than the type. The pinnules are daintier and sharply pointed (acute). Bulbils are produced underneath along the rachis. Some forms have cut pinnules and begin to merge with the Divisilobum group, but such names as 'Acutilobo-proliferum' are meaningless. At one time 'acutilobum' and 'proliferum' appear to have been interchangeable, but in the final analysis it is best to stick to group names unless cultivar status is reliably attained.

P.s. Congestum group. Dwarf forms for the rock garden, only nine inches or so in height, with overlapping pinnae. Under the current rules for naming garden plants, the fact that the name covers plants that come true from spores entitles them to cultivar status as *P.s.* 'Congestum'. Those rules are currently under widespread attack for inconsistency of definition, so this is a name with an uncertain future.

P.s. Cristatum group. Forms with varying degrees of cresting at the ends of the pinnae, sometimes with quite large terminal crests.

P.s. 'Cristato-Gracile'. The name and the variety are very old and accurately refer to an erect-growing, fairly attenuated plant (under two feet), dark green in colour, and with crested pinnae.

P.s. Cristato-Pinnulum'. This variety is occasionally offered, but the plants involved are from two to three feet high, whereas Reginald Kaye suggests that little more than half that height should be expected.

These last two forms have now been absorbed into the Percristatum group, which is a sensible move, avoiding as it does any worries about correct naming. However, it seems sad that the status of so many ferns has been allowed to degenerate through muddle so that umbrella names are in some cases greeted with positive relief.

P.s. Divisilobum group. This is a section of the species in which are many diverse forms, a few of which have cultivar status. They have large, tripinnate fronds that can sometimes be quadripinnate, and the pinnules are finely and lacily cut.

The following may be legitimately and even probably better written as Divisilobum group 'Laxum', 'Mrs Goffey', etc.

P.s. 'Divisilobum Laxum' is a frothy but neat fern with the 'thumbs' lying wide of the 'mittens' and alongside the rachis. Beyond them is much dividing

Polystichum setiferum 'Divisilobum Laxum'. King's Gatchell, Ottery St Mary, Devon. *John Kelly*

of the pinnules.

P.s. 'Divisilobum Herrenhausen' is, in my opinion, a name rather too often seen on non-divisilobe forms, particularly in Dutch nurseries, for credence to be given to catalogue descriptions. The plants should be seen first.

P.s. 'Divisilobum Mrs Goffey'. Once known as 'Mrs Goffey's Very Fine Variety' in the days when names were more poetic and less governed by rules, this is a rare plant that appears from time to time in lists and is a filigreed, tri- to quadripinnate form much sought after by fern enthusiasts. It is just as easy to grow as any other, however.

P.s. 'Divisilobum Iveryanum' has finely divided fronds and a large crest at the tip and at the end of each pinna. Other plants have been sold under this name in the past.

P.s. Plumoso-Divisilobum group. These ferns are so finely divided that their degree of pinnateness (in fact they are quadripinnate) is almost indistinguishable. The plants make what look like clumps of green ostrich plumes and are about as feathery.

P.s. 'Plumoso-Divisilobum Baldwinii' (or Plumoso-Divisilobum group 'Baldwinii') is even more finely divided into silky, hair-like filaments. Although it is perfectly hardy, its beauty is best appreciated in a conservatory or cold glasshouse.

P.s. 'Pulcherrimum Bevis'. Previously believed to be a form of *P. aculeatum*. It is another finely-divided fern of silky texture. The filaments are long and those near the tips of the fronds come together and hang as separate tassels. Its colour is dark green. As it can be readily propagated vegetatively, it appears reasonably frequently in nursery lists, but other, even more stunning varieties, such as 'Druery', which has three-inch filaments, are in private collections.

P. tsus-simense
Japan, China, Korea. A neat, dark green fern, only eighteen inches high. It is hardy and enjoys a shady spot in the rock garden or border.

SELAGINELLAS

Selaginellas are not ferns, but are relatives of them. They are sometimes called spikemosses. I am including a short account of them, not because they are ever likely to be grown at all widely in the open garden in Britain, but because they are a group of plants that are about to become of greater interest than they have been before. This is in part because of advances in horticultural understanding and in part a result of the undeniably high standard of living that we now enjoy, which allows so many of us to contemplate building conservatories – something we would not have begun to do a couple of decades ago.

Selaginellas are plants of warm places, but by no means all of them are Tropical in origin, or even Sub-Tropical. Two species, one of which is in commercial cultivation, are of proven hardiness, and some others are quite possibly about to surprise us and prove hardy too. Modern gardeners are less likely than their predecessors to take what 'experts' say for granted, and a spirit of experiment is abroad.

I have chosen to illustrate the genus with a photograph of the Mexican *Selaginella pallescens* (syn. *S. cuspidata*), which is, frankly, tender. However, its beauty so sums up what selaginellas are all about and so demonstrates their attractiveness to those who like ferns, that I hope I shall be forgiven for seeming to suggest the attainable.

Perhaps the best use of the following species is as ground cover beneath other plants in an airy conservatory which does not become dank. Selaginellas like shade and moisture, but they hate stagnant air and staleness. As companions for ferns in such a comfortable situation they are superb and provide an element

Selaginella pallescens. Fairchild Tropical Garden, Coral Gables, Miami, Florida.
Nicola Kelly

of exotic interest that is precisely right for conservatories, much of whose space tends to be wasted on brobdingnagian pelargoniums instead of being devoted to more worthy occupants.

S. braunii
China. An upright, ferny plant with dark green, hard foliage. It has a very good chance of turning out to be hardy, even though it is treated as a tropical plant at Kew.

S. emiliana (sometimes written as *S. emmeliana*)
A synonym of *S. pallescens*, a tender species from Mexico, which likes a light, airy position. There are pink-tinted and golden forms.

S. kraussiana
A trailing species from South Africa, with stems up to a foot long. The foliage is bright green and makes a dense mat, often used under greenhouse staging. Many escapes, resulting in successful adaptations to outdoor life in Britain, and

not by any means always in the soft south, have led to a growing appreciation of this plant's future in gardens. It may not create the media splash that a new rose does, but in many ways it is more exciting.

S.k. aurea has golden foliage. *S.k. brownii* is a congested, dwarf form from the Azores, which could well be hardy in the south and west.

S. apoda (syn. *S. apus*)
North America. A bun-forming treasure for growing in a pot in a cold greenhouse or frame. It is not hardy, but needs the minimum of heat to keep it in good health.

S. martensii var. *watsoniana*
Another Mexican, with an upright habit (the species itself is decumbent). Its ferny foliage is up to eighteen inches high and bright green.

THELYPTERIS

T. palustris
Britain, Europe, North America, China, Japan. An unusual fern with short sterile fronds and much longer fertile ones, which appear a month later. The fronds are individual, arising from a creeping rhizome, and fertile ones may be as much as five feet tall, but are usually between three and four. They are pinnate, the pinnae deeply pinnatifid, light green. Semi-persistent.

The plant is a lime-hater, but is otherwise easy to grow in a moist, partly shaded position, where it grows strongly and spreads without becoming a nuisance. In moist soils it will tolerate full sun.

WOODWARDIA

W. radicans. Chain fern
A magnificent fern from the south of Europe and the Canary Islands, part of a relict flora that once stretched from Tenerife to the Black Sea. It has superb fronds, up to six feet long, but usually about five, which arch so strongly that each tip, where a singularly large bulbil occurs, is firmly pressed against the ground. They are pinnate, the pinnae deeply pinnatifid, glossy green and leathery.

It is hardy in mild areas in shady, moist places sheltered from the wind. If you only have one plant, it is better off in a cold house or conservatory until you can peg a bulbil down and root it – a simple procedure. If the young plant is established in a pot it can then be planted out.

Appendix

Pests and Diseases

THERE ARE two cardinal facts to be remembered concerning the health of ferns; they are comparatively rarely attacked by pests and seldom suffer from disease; and most sprays are dangerous to them. By their very nature fern fronds, especially deciduous ones, begin to look a little tattered by autumn in any case.

As with all plants, good cultivation promotes health. A short digression from ferns may serve to illustrate this quite strongly. My wife's father lives in an area which is notoriously bad for growing roses. I am quite sure that the chief pollutants of the summer air are blackspot and rust spores. For some years he struggled with debilitated bushes that became partly defoliated every year and bore few blooms, until one year he pruned them ruthlessly to ground level and shovelled a three-inch layer of stable manure over them.

Being but a reluctant gardener, he then forgot to spray them for the whole spring and summer. Nevertheless, by September there was barely a blemish to be seen on the luxuriant foliage, and the flowers were abundant and magnificent.

Ferns similarly appreciate good food. You may think that a fern in a crack in a rock is doing well enough, but go and find a plant of the same species, fatly smug on crumbly-floury generations of leaf mould, and you will see the difference between a dwarf and a giant. The latter plant may well have had a mouthful of its substance lost to a passing slug, but it will hardly show, whereas the smaller plant could hardly afford to lose that much of itself.

This is not to say that your plants in their rock-garden crevices will be that much more vulnerable. You will, if you have followed the description of how to make a rock garden, have realised that such places provide ample nutriment. It is, nevertheless, a fundamental precept of fern-growing that true plant food, provided in Nature's own way, is the best preventive medicine.

To this end, peat is inferior to leafmould. Peat is a very good soil conditioner indeed, but at the risk of repeating myself I must emphasise that it contains no plant foods until it breaks down. A mixture of peat and leafmould is first class, but the peat should be omitted for those ferns that do not like it. For ferns that must have an acid soil, such as blechnums, use the peat/leafmould mixture but make sure that the leafmould is not from beech trees, as they concentrate lime in their tissues.

The slug army is not universally deployed. Some gardens are quite free of them. The twenty-acre so-called Sub-Tropical garden at Abbotsbury, in Dorset, England, is astonishingly free of them and I can honestly say that the only slugs I saw there in twelve years were in the frames. The reason for this was that a pride of up to twenty peacocks, a rich population of wild birds, and umpteen pheasants (making hearty breakfasts, like all condemned creatures) saw to it that slugs and snails stood no chance.

The surest way to encourage slugs is to keep a cat. The birds that will eat the slugs are frightened away. If you are a cat lover, as I am, you must either have a bigger garden and restrict yourself to just one cat, or learn to live with slugs.

Slugs are unpredictable in their attacks on ferns. Reginald Kaye says that spring is the most vulnerable time, when the young fronds are unfurling. I have found this to be so with aspleniums, but the lady fern is very liable to damage in summer, especially where the fronds trail along the ground. Any fern can be attacked, but those with leathery fronds or with hairy foliage usually escape.

It would be entirely wrong to give the impression that slugs are a serious enemy of ferns. Among so few predators and problems slugs are significant, but the damage they do is minimal. After all, plants that have evolved to live on the woodland floor and in the moistest places must be equipped to cope with such things as slugs and snails whose favourite places they also are.

It is, therefore, better to live with the slugs than to lay pellets for them. Even if you cover the pellets so that birds cannot find them, they still pose a risk. Birds are actually unlikely to take the pellets themselves and are far more likely to swallow a slug, made dozy by the pellet it has ingested, but not yet dried up and unattractive to the bird. Two mallard ducks will do the work of many kilograms of slug pellets!

In the conservatory and greenhouse, it is a different story. In such artificial environments slugs and other pests, such as woodlice, can do a lot of damage if they are allowed to proliferate. Here again, common sense is the rule, and sensible hygiene will prevent much damage occurring. Cold frames and places under the staging, where your sporelings are being raised, need to be scrupulously clean and free from all debris. Woodlice are partial to infant plants of whatever sort, and slugs enjoy a salad of baby ferns. You can use slug pellets in the indoor environments, in fact they may be considered essential; but don't let the children come into contact with them.

Our friends the birds have their own lives to lead, so we must be prepared for them to get on with making their nests as best they may. Nothing is quite as good for a snug lining as moss, and birds scratch away at it until they have soil-free pieces of the right size for carrying. Unfortunately, they are very likely to scratch up young ferns just making their way in the mossy environment. They will also make a mess when looking for insect food for their broods and can leave a diminutive fern, roots uppermost, to dry up in an hour or two. Vigilance is the only answer. If you try using black cotton you will only wreck the ferns when you come to remove it, as they will have grown through the strands.

Insect pests are not a major problem on the whole. Aphids seldom attack in strength, if at all, and you will probably find yourself living with them, too. However, take care when spraying aphids on other plants in a mixed border, as sprays that are harmless on shrubs and perennials are highly likely to damage ferns. Use derris for the ferns, but do not apply it during the hours when bees are operating, as it may drift and poison them.

Vine weevils are a nuisance. They do not, on the whole, damage ferns themselves, except under glass, but it is the companion plants of ferns that can suffer most. The adults climb up the stems of rhododendrons and chew holes in the edges of the leaves, producing a characteristic, deckle-edged appearance, and seedlings of such things as candelabra primulas are eaten off at ground level by the grubs. Under glass, they may attack young ferns or succulent young fronds. Once again, hygiene is the cure and the prevention. Make certain that no rubbish, dead leaves, or bits of wood are lying about, where the insects may hide up. In the open, put grease-bands round the stems of affected shrubs and dress the root area thoroughly with a contact insecticide in powder form. Vine weevils are not often present on alkaline soils, but are a common pest where rhododendrons and camellias are grown. All members of the Primulaceae are vulnerable, but ferns in the open are not usually attacked directly.

A leaf-borer sometimes channels its way along the midribs of some ferns, particularly the lady fern. Above its progress the frond turns brown, but if you cut the affected part away, including a little of the healthy frond just to make sure you have caught the invader, all should be well.

The glasshouse environment is such that it encourages plant diseases, and ferns can fall prey to some, but they are, as the Victorians found, tough customers even in such a botanically insanitary atmosphere. In the open there is only one disease that is specific to ferns, and it is the only one that need concern us.

Fern rust is especially prevalent in the genus *Asplenium*, especially in mild, damp climates. The undersides of fronds develop brown patches which bear spores. They are easily distinguishable from sporangia, as they are irregular in shape and distribution. Curiously enough, it is a disease which is more prevalent in ferns growing near or with conifers. The affected fronds should be removed and burnt.

Suppliers of Ferns

The following list covers suppliers in the United Kingdom only. All of them operate by mail order.

TREE FERNS (*Dicksonia* and *Cyathea* species)

Architectural Plants, Cooks Farm, Nuthurst, Horsham, W. Sussex, RH13 6LH.
The Palm Farm, Thornton Hall Gardens, Thornton Curtis, Nr. Ulceby, South Humberside, DN39 6XF.

HARDY FERNS

Apple Court, Hordle Lane, Lymington, Hants., SO41 0HU.
Blooms of Bressingham, Diss, Norfolk, IP22 2AB.
Fibrex Nurseries Ltd., Honeybourne Road, Pebworth, Nr. Stratford-upon-Avon, Warwicks., CV37 8XT.
Holden Clough Nursery, Holden, Bolton by Boland, Clitheroe, Lancs., BB7 4PF.
Reginald Kaye Ltd., Waithman Nurseries, Silverdale, Carnforth, Lancs., LA5 OTY.
J. & D. Marston, 'Culag', Green Lane, Nafferton, Driffield, East Yorkshire.

Bibliography

EVANS, ALFRED. *The Peat Garden and its Plants*. Dent, 1974.
HARPER, P. and MCGOURTY, F. *Perennials*. H. P. Books, Tucson, Arizona, USA, 1985.
KAYE, REGINALD. *Hardy Ferns*. Faber, 1968.
LORD, A. (ed.) *The Plant Finder*. Hardy Plant Society, 1987 *et seq*.
PHILLIPS, ROGER. *Grasses, Ferns, Mosses and Lichens of Great Britain and Ireland*. Pan, 1980.
ROYAL HORTICULTURAL SOCIETY. *Dictionary of Gardening*. 4 vols. (1965) and Supp. (1969).
RUSH, RICHARD. *A Guide to Hardy Ferns*. British Pteridological Society, 1984.
THOMAS, GRAHAM STUART. *Perennial Garden Plants*. Dent, 3rd edition 1990.

Glossary

Acute. Sharply pointed.
Alternate. Arranged alternately on a midrib (of pinnae or pinnules).
Annulus. A ring of moisture-sensitive cells in the wall of the sporangium. Part of the spore-releasing mechanism.
Antheridium. The male reproductive organ on the prothallus.
Archegonium. The female reproductive organ on the prothallus.
Auricle. An ear-like or ear-lobe-like projection on a frond, usually at the base.
Bipinnate. A condition in which the pinnae are themselves pinnate.
Blade. The leafy part of a frond.
Bulbil. A bulb-like plantlet, usually occurring near the rachis.
Chromosome. All living cells contain thread- or blob-like bodies that consist of strings of genes. They are the structures that determine heredity. There are always the same number in any cell of any member of a species, except for the germ cells, which have half the number, and in the case of abnormalities.
Cordate. Heart-shaped.
Corymbose. Of a tasselled, tightly bunched crest.
Deciduous. (Of fronds.) Falling in autumn or in winter before new ones are formed.
Decumbent. Reclining on the ground, but with ascending tips.
Dentate. Toothed.
Digitate. Of crests like the fingers of a hand.
Dimorphic. Of fronds of which two types, sterile and fertile, are borne on an individual plant.
Diploid. Having the 2n, or full number of chromosomes (see haploid)
Entire. Not divided, toothed, or waved.
Epiphytic. Growing on trees, but not parasitically.
Gametophyte. In ferns, the prothallus; the gamete-bearing state of a species.
Glabrous. Smooth.
Glaucous. With a blue cast or bloom.
Haploid. Having half the chromosome number for the species.
Indusium. The membrane covering the sorus.
Lanceolate. A frond that is shaped like the head of a lance, broadest below the middle.

Linear. Long and slender.
Lobe. A distinct portion of a frond that itself may or may not be subdivided.
Muricate. With raised wrinkles.
Oblanceolate. Shaped like the head of a lance, but broadest above the middle.
Obovate. Egg-shaped, broadest above the middle.
Ovate. Egg-shaped, broadest below the middle.
Pinna. A primary division of the frond blade.
Pinnate. Divided into pinnae.
Pinnatifid. Not quite pinnate; the divisions do not reach the midrib.
Pinnule. A division of a pinna.
Prothallus. The generation of a fern that arises from the germination of a spore; the gametophyte.
Quadripinnate. The pinnules are divided, and then the divisions are themselves divided.
Rachis. The midrib of the blade.
Ramose. A variation in which the blade branches repeatedly near its junction with the stem.
Saxatile. Growing among rocks.
Serrate. With saw-like teeth.
Sessile. Without a stalk.
Simple. In the strict sense of a frond, undivided. Also used loosely in this book to denote a relatively simple appearance.
Sinuate. With a wavy edge.
Sorus. A cluster of sporangia.
Sporangium. An individual spore-bearing organ.
Spore. An asexual reproductive cell.
Sporophyte. The fern plant as we know it. The asexual generation of the fern.
Tripinnate. The pinnules are fully divided.

The British Pteridological Society

The Society was founded in 1891 and continues as a focus for fern enthusiasts, organising talks, field meetings and exchanges of plants and spores. Both the spore exchange and the *Fern Gazette* (published annually) are of international interest. Address: c/o The British Museum (Natural History), Cromwell Road, London SW7 5BD, England.

Index

Numbers in italics refer to illustrations